Anticorruption in Transition 3

Who Is Succeeding . . . and Why?

James H. Anderson
Cheryl W. Gray

THE WORLD BANK

ISBN-10: 0-8213-6692-0
ISBN-13: 978-0-8213-6692-9
eISBN: 0-8213-6693-9
DOI: 10.1596/978-0-8213-6692-9

Library of Congress Cataloging-in-Publication Data has been applied for.

Contents

Tables

Acknowledgments

This report was prepared by James Anderson and Cheryl Gray, supported by excellent research assistance from Laura Lanteri. We are grateful to the Office of the Chief Economist, Europe and Central Asia, for support of this study. The report benefited from comments provided by the peer reviewers—Daniel Kaufmann, Stephen Knack, Sanjay Pradhan, and Alan Rousso. Other insights were provided by Arup Banerji, Sunil Bhattacharya, Paul Bermingham, Sudharshan Canagarajah, Kevin Casey, Roland Clarke, Yelena Dobrolyubova, Monica Dorhoi, Anca Dumitrescu, Carlos Ferreira, Hans Jurgen Gruss, Gohar Gyulumyan, Elene Imnadze, Ivailo Izvorski, Felipe Jaramillo, Leszek Kasek, Pascale Kervyn, Kathy Lalazarian, John Litwack, Chris Lovelace, Ali Mansoor, Anton Marcincin, Massimo Mastruzzi, Pradeep Mitra, Saumya Mitra, Gerald Ollivier, Rosalinda Quintanilla, Martin Raiser, Francesca Recanatini, Andriy Storozhuk, Piet Van Heesewijk, and Tony Verheijen. We are also grateful to Marinette Guevara and Erlinda Inglis for help in preparing the manuscript.

This report uses data from the European Bank for Reconstruction and Development-World Bank Business Environment and Enterprise Performance Survey (BEEPS) extensively, and the authors wish to acknowledge the people who worked to ensure that the survey collected data of high quality in a consistent manner, especially Sam Fankhauser and Alan Rousso of EBRD; Savvas Kyriakides and the staff of Synovate; John Nasir and Jorge Meza (EAU); and James Anderson, Laura Lanteri, and Derek Fears (ECSPE). Finally, we wish to thank the more than 20,000 enterprise managers who have given their time to this survey over the years.

Acronyms and Abbreviations

ACT1	Anticorruption in Transition: A Contribution to the Policy Debate
ACT2	Anticorruption in Transition 2: Corruption in Enterprise-State Interactions in Europe and Central Asia, 1999–2002
BEEPS	Business Environment and Enterprise Performance Survey
CEFIR	Center for Economic and Financial Research
CIS	Commonwealth of Independent States
CPIA	Country Policy and Institutional Assessment
EAU	Enterprise Analysis Unit
EBRD	European Bank for Reconstruction and Development
ECA	Europe and Central Asia
ESCPE	Economic Management and Poverty Reduction Department, Europe and Central Asia, World Bank
EU	European Union
GDP	Gross Domestic Product
GRECO	Group of States Against Corruption
IMF	International Monetary Fund
INDEM	Information Science for Democracy
OECD	Organisation for Economic Co-operation and Development
SEE	Southeastern Europe
SPAI	Stability Pact Anticorruption Initiative
TI-CPI	Transparency International Corruption Perceptions Index
TI-GCB	Transparency International Global Corruption Barometer
TTFSE	Trade and Transport Facilitation in Southeast Europe
VAT	Value-added Tax

Country abbreviations used in figures and tables:
Alb = Albania; Arm = Armenia; Aze = Azerbaijan; Bel = Belarus; BiH = Bosnia and Herzegovina; Bul = Bulgaria; Cro = Croatia; Cze = Czech Republic; Esp = Spain; Est = Estonia; Geo = Georgia; Ger = Germany; Gre = Greece; Hun = Hungary; Ire = Ireland; Kaz = Kazakhstan; Kyr = Kyrgyz Republic; Lat = Latvia; Lit = Lithuania; Mac = FYR Macedonia; Mol = Moldova; Pol = Poland; Por = Portugal; Rom = Romania; Rus = Russian Federation; SAM = Serbia and Montenegro; Slk = Slovak Republic; Sln = Slovenia; Taj = Tajikistan; Tur = Turkey; Ukr = Ukraine; Uzb = Uzbekistan.

Executive Summary

In the 16 years since the start of transition in the former socialist economies of Europe and Central Asia, few issues have risen as rapidly in visibility as corruption. Reforms in the early 1990s were focused on macroeconomic stabilization, price and trade liberalization, privatization, and establishment of the legal foundations of a market economy. Institutional reforms to ensure accountability, transparency, and public sector effectiveness often took a back seat. But while corruption was barely mentioned at the start of the 1990s, by the end of the decade it had come to be recognized as a central challenge to progress in many countries in the region. Corruption has been an important issue in the discussions surrounding EU enlargement, has figured prominently in political campaigns, and has been a key concern of citizens, businesses, and international organizations alike. Leading reformers have in turn paid greater attention to governance issues generally and corruption in particular in recent years.

This report is the third in a series of studies[1] since 2000 that examines patterns and trends in corruption in business-government interactions in Europe and Central Asia and the progress achieved by countries in addressing it. All three studies have drawn on data from a large-scale survey of enterprises undertaken jointly by the European Bank for Reconstruction and Development and the World Bank—the EBRD-World Bank Business Environment and Enterprise Performance Survey (BEEPS). More than 20,000 firms have been interviewed over three rounds of the survey (in 1999, 2002, and 2005), yielding in-depth cross-country and time-series data on many aspects of the business environment,[2] including the frequency and cost of bribes paid by different types of businesses in various interactions with government.

Continued improvements in many countries

The key finding of this report is that in quite a few of the transition countries of Europe and Central Asia, firms reported a smaller incidence of corruption in 2005 than they had three years earlier, continuing the trend established by earlier surveys.[3] In many countries, firms are paying bribes less frequently and in smaller relative amounts (as a share of firm revenues) than in the past, and they view corruption as less of a problem for the operation and growth of their business than in 2002 (see Figure 1). Among countries showing the most dramatic improvements are Georgia and the Slovak Republic, where committed leaders are implementing strong programs of economic and institutional reform and firm-level bribery has fallen substantially. Romania and Bulgaria are also seeing some success, which bodes well for their entry into the European Union, and improvements are evident along some dimensions in Moldova, Tajikistan, Ukraine, and Latvia (an early leader in tackling corruption), as well as several other countries.

Improvement can be found in every subregion, though not in every country. Firms reported increases in the frequency of bribery in Albania, Serbia and Montenegro, and the Kyrgyz Republic (which had a revolution right at the time of the survey), and corruption was seen as a bigger problem for business in 2005 than in 2002 in Azerbaijan, the Czech Republic, and Russia. Albania and the Kyrgyz Republic continued in 2005, as in 2002, to have the worst corruption indicators of the 33 countries surveyed.

For the first time in 2004/5, the BEEPS also was conducted in a number of nontransition countries, including five European comparators: Greece, Ireland, Germany, Portugal, and Spain. A sixth comparator country, Turkey, has been included in all rounds of the survey. The results confirm the widespread assumption that corruption tends to be worse in transition countries than in Western Europe, indicating that most transition countries—including the eight new members of the European Union in Central and Eastern Europe—still have a way to go in improving accountability in government. However, along some dimensions of corruption the nontransition European comparators—most notably Greece and occasionally Portugal, Turkey, and the eastern part of Germany—fared worse than many transition countries.

Firm characteristics, institutions, and political systems

Corruption does not affect all firms equally. New, private, domestically owned firms are likely to pay the most in bribes (as a share of revenues)

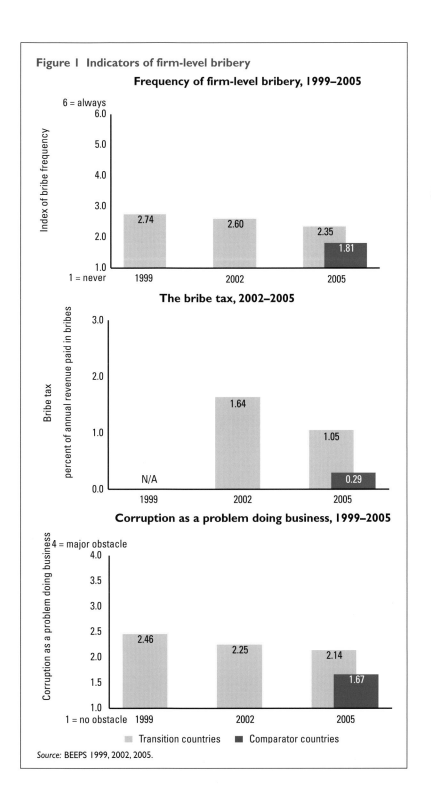

Figure 1 Indicators of firm-level bribery

Frequency of firm-level bribery, 1999–2005

Index of bribe frequency

6 = always

- 6.0
- 5.0
- 4.0
- 3.0
- 2.0
- 1.0

1 = never

1999: 2.74
2002: 2.60
2005: 2.35 / 1.81

The bribe tax, 2002–2005

Bribe tax — percent of annual revenue paid in bribes

- 3.0
- 2.0
- 1.0
- 0.0

1999: N/A
2002: 1.64
2005: 1.05 / 0.29

Corruption as a problem doing business, 1999–2005

Corruption as a problem doing business

4 = major obstacle

- 4.0
- 3.5
- 3.0
- 2.5
- 2.0
- 1.5
- 1.0

1 = no obstacle

1999: 2.46
2002: 2.25
2005: 2.14 / 1.67

▢ Transition countries   ■ Comparator countries

Source: BEEPS 1999, 2002, 2005.

and pay bribes the most frequently (Figure 2). Foreign-owned firms pay less in bribes, as do larger or older firms, state-owned firms, and firms in smaller towns or rural areas. This uneven incidence of bribery threatens to undermine the growth of small and medium enterprises, which are the engines of economic growth, diversification, and private-sector development throughout the region.

Corruption continues to be higher in countries where policies and institutions are weak. While richer countries tend to have better institutions and lower corruption, there is no evidence that faster economic growth reduces corruption in the short run. Indeed, state capture may be exacerbated by faster growth, particularly if such growth is driven largely by natural resource sectors as in some countries in the region.

Patterns of corruption are more complex in countries where transition is still at a relatively early stage. Firms in countries such as Belarus and Uzbekistan report lower levels of bribery in the BEEPS than one might expect based on indicators generated by experts. Such discrepancies could reflect different definitions of corruption: Open bribery may be limited due to the small size of the private sector and the stronger control environment, but corruption may still be widespread, manifest through direct state control of economic activity for the benefit of elites. Alternatively, actual bribery may be higher than firms are willing to report in an atmosphere where civil liberties are constrained. In either case,

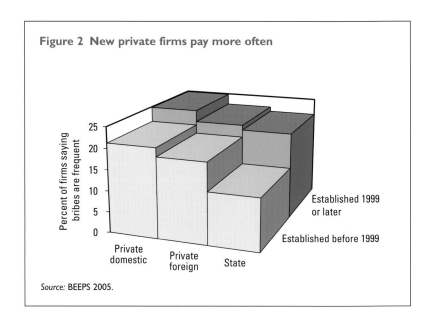

Figure 2 New private firms pay more often

Percent of firms saying bribes are frequent

Private domestic   Private foreign   State

Established 1999 or later

Established before 1999

Source: BEEPS 2005.

fundamental progress in improving governance is unlikely without reforms to foster more open, transparent, and competitive economic and political systems.

Progress in some areas, but not others

The generalized story of improvement in transition countries becomes more fragmented when focusing on specific types of enterprise-state interactions. Trends in corruption related to taxes, customs, and business licensing tend to be favorable, but trends in other areas, notably government procurement and the judiciary, do not show improvement (Figure 3). The disparity in performance is not random: Areas that have received the most attention from reformers have typically shown more improvement, while those that are the most complicated or are beset with conflicting objectives have shown less.

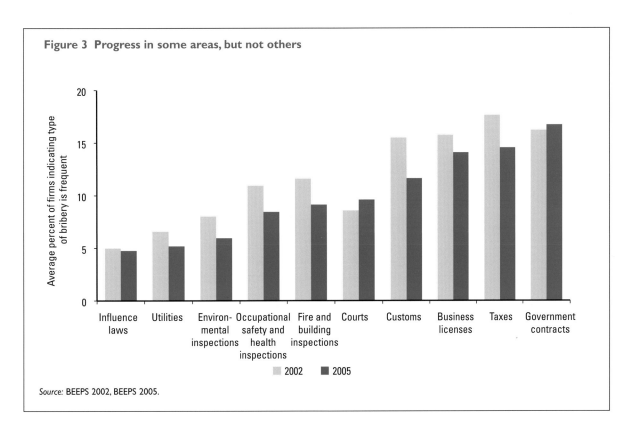

Figure 3 Progress in some areas, but not others

Y-axis: Average percent of firms indicating type of bribery is frequent

Legend: 2002, 2005

Source: BEEPS 2002, BEEPS 2005.

Taxation has been one of the most visible areas of reform in recent years. Chronic tax evasion in the 1990s was driven in part by high and steeply progressive rate structures, and several countries in Europe and Central Asia took the lead world-wide in moving to low- or flat-rate income taxes in the late 1990s and early 2000s. These tend to be the same countries that have seen the largest declines in both corruption in tax administration and tax evasion. In the Slovak Republic, for example, a comprehensive tax and benefit reform did not result in significantly lower collections despite a decrease in rates. The BEEPS confirms that Slovak firms say they are evading taxes less often than in the past and that bribery in tax administration has declined. More generally, countries with less burdensome tax regimes tend to have lower levels of corruption in tax administration.

Two other areas where reforms are leading to lower levels of corruption in some transition countries are customs and business regulation. In southeast Europe, a multinational effort to streamline customs procedures and improve efficiency at border crossings is reducing clearance times at the borders while also helping to lower corruption. Indeed, the southeast Europe region showed more improvement from 2002 to 2005 in levels of bribery at customs than any other region. In the area of business regulation, reforms to reduce the burden on firms have included one-stop shops; streamlined, one-day business registration; and limits on the number of inspections per year. Cross-country evidence shows that countries with less burdensome regulatory systems tend to have lower levels of corruption. Most transition countries have seen improvements in the area of inspections, while the story for business licensing and permits is somewhat more mixed.

One area that has not seen overall improvement in firms' assessment is the courts. Only a handful of countries saw significant reductions in corruption in the judiciary from 2002 to 2005, and a similar number saw increases. Judicial reforms tended to take a back seat in the 1990s to other areas of institutional reform, although this is now changing, particularly in EU candidate countries. Where attention was given, judicial independence was typically a higher priority than accountability or capacity. Establishing independence without ensuring accountability can open the door to widespread corruption, which appears to have occurred in some settings. The continued large disparity in judicial integrity between transition and comparator countries and the lack of improvement in the former suggest that this relatively neglected area of reform should receive greater attention.

Progress is also lagging, according to firms, in the area of government procurement. While a few countries saw significant improvements from 2002 to 2005, corruption appears to have worsened in others. As the region continues to develop and larger investment projects become more feasible, the temptation for corruption in government procurement will get even worse. Even in the most advanced countries with sophisticated procurement systems, corruption scandals often surround procurement transactions. Indeed, some of the European comparators have higher levels of unofficial payments related to procurement than several of the transition countries. Improving procurement systems—focusing on transparency, competition, and standardization—must be a key priority for governance reforms in the coming years.

Finally, many transition countries have adopted cross-cutting legislation that requires top officials to publicly disclose their income or assets and restricts the scope for conflict of interest. Many have also adopted freedom-of-information laws, and some have strengthened systems of financial audit or established anticorruption commissions. Often these laws are elements of national anticorruption strategies. Anecdotes of successes and failures abound, and critics sometimes deride these initiatives as superficial. Reforms in some areas—such as financial audit and control—appear to have helped to reduce corruption, while reforms in other areas—such as asset monitoring—have a more mixed record, possibly due to variation in design and implementation. One striking finding is that current levels of corruption are more closely correlated with the anticorruption institutions in place in 1995 than they are with those put in place more recently, a reminder that progress takes time.

External and internal drivers of change

As corruption becomes ever more prominent in the league of development ills, the importance of monitoring corruption and the institutional frameworks being employed to fight it becomes ever greater. For the transition countries of Europe and Central Asia, such monitoring has shown that policy and institutional reforms can have dramatic effects. Throughout much of the region, the past few years have seen strong economic growth and accelerating reforms in economic policies, public institutions, and the business environment. Firms, by and large, are reporting lower levels of corruption than they have in the past.

The trend is favorable but by no means irreversible. Even the world's ~~most advanced countries must be con~~stantly on the watch to control corruption. Continued progress in transition countries will require persistent attention to weaknesses and to new challenges as they arise. Greater attention needs to be paid to judicial and procurement reforms, among others. Regulation of conflicts of interest remains weak in many countries, and systems of asset monitoring vary greatly in implementation. Improvements in financial audit and control seem to be having some effect in reducing corruption, but they need further strengthening. Excessive immunities, the least improved area of anticorruption policies in the past decade, continue to render some politicians untouchable.

What forces have underpinned successes? First, the external environment—most notably the goal of joining the European Union—has had a major impact in stimulating anticorruption efforts in accession candidates such as Romania and Bulgaria. Indeed, the desire to meet European standards is a motivator for governance improvements far beyond the borders of the EU.

Second, the internal political system inevitably defines the incentives and sets the boundaries within which policies and institutions are formed. The opening up of closed political systems may lead to an expansion of some forms of corruption in the short term, but over time more political and economic competition helps foster the transparency and accountability that is essential for controlling corruption.

Finally, individuals matter, and strong leadership is essential in shaping and pushing reform. Every country that has achieved some success on the anticorruption front has had leaders who have tenaciously pushed the reform agenda. Romanian leaders recently strengthened the asset declaration law and have worked to support prosecutors who are keen to tackle corruption. Key Slovak leaders were instrumental in pursuing far-reaching tax and budget reforms. The Georgian government has doggedly pursued fundamental reforms in many areas since the Rose Revolution in late 2003. Leaders cannot expect to eliminate corruption, but the experience with reforms in Europe and Central Asia shows that leaders with strong commitment, courage, and support can make important strides in a relatively short period of time.

Notes

1. The first two studies were *Anticorruption in Transition: A Contribution to the Policy Debate* (2000) and *Anticorruption in Transition 2: Corruption in Enterprise-State Interactions 1999-2002* (2004).

2. For more information on the BEEPS, see www.worldbank/eca/econ or www.worldbank/eca/governance .

3. Neither the BEEPS nor this report address corruption in the delivery of public services to individuals and households, and patterns and trends in corruption affecting households are not necessarily the same as those affecting businesses. There is some evidence, however, that the favorable trends in firm-level corruption between 2002 and 2005 may apply also to corruption faced by households. Transparency International's *Global Corruption Barometer* (TI-GCB) surveyed citizens in 20 of the countries covered by the BEEPS. Average responses related to health, education, and the police—the three sectors that households are most likely to encounter—showed an overall decline in perceptions of corruption between 2004 and 2005. Country-level changes were correlated with changes in bribe frequency and bribe tax as measured by the BEEPS, driven largely by Georgia, which shows improvement in both the BEEPS and the TI-GCB (Transparency International, 2004, 2005).

1

Introduction

THIS REPORT IS THE THIRD IN A SERIES OF DETAILED STUDIES PREPARED by the World Bank on patterns and trends in corruption in the transition countries of Europe and Central Asia (ECA). The first study, *Anticorruption in Transition: A Contribution to the Policy Debate (ACT 1)*, was published in 2000 for the World Bank-IMF Annual Meetings in Prague, and the second, *Anticorruption in Transition 2: Corruption in Enterprise-State Interactions in Europe and Central Asia 1999–2002 (ACT 2)*, was published in early 2004. All three reports are based on the findings of cross-country surveys of enterprises, the EBRD-World Bank Business Environment and Enterprise Performance Surveys (BEEPS), as described in Box 1.1. Taken together, this work provides an in-depth look at how corruption in business-government interactions is changing in the transition countries and what factors might be influencing those trends.

Corruption has received ever-expanding attention in the past decade, although this was not the case in the early stages of the transition process. For the first few years of transition in the early 1990s, the twin challenges of dismantling communism and installing the basic building blocks of democratic free-market systems occupied reformers. But it was not long until a sense of injustice and disillusionment with the transition process began to emerge among a large segment of the population. The process of designing wholly new legal and regulatory frameworks, as needed for a market economy, provided wide-ranging opportunities for newly emerging elites to gain personal advantages. The privatization process in some transition countries was seen by many as unfair and corrupt, but countries that did not privatize as quickly did not escape the problem, as managers of state-owned firms were often seen as illegally siphoning off state-owned assets for personal uses. With the controls of the communist

Box 1.1 The Business Environment and Enterprise Performance Survey

The EBRD-World Bank Business Environment and Enterprise Performance Survey (BEEPS), a joint initiative of EBRD and the World Bank, has been carried out in three rounds in 1999, 2002, and 2005. The survey covers 27 countries, including Turkey and all transition countries of Central and Eastern Europe and the former Soviet Union (except Turkmenistan). More than 20,000 firms have been interviewed—about 4,500 in 1999, 6,000 in 2002, and almost 10,000 in 2005. Based on face-to-face interviews with firm managers and owners, BEEPS is designed to generate comparative measurements on many aspects of the business environment, which can then be related to specific firm characteristics and firm performance. BEEPS3 in 2005 added several new features, including a panel subsample of 1,462 firms (interviewed both in 2002 and 2005), and a "manufacturing overlay" of 1,715 firms in seven countries to allow in-depth analysis of particular subsectors. (To maintain comparability across countries, the manufacturing overlay was not included in the analysis for this report.) An extension of BEEPS to several nontransition countries in Europe and Asia provides a broader set of comparators. The nontransition comparator countries used in this study include Germany, Greece, Ireland, Portugal, Spain, and Turkey.

The BEEPS used an identical sampling approach in all three years, with the sectoral breakdown of firms in each country determined by their relative contribution to GDP. Farms and regulated firms (such as banking, power, rail, and water) were excluded. The breakdown of the BEEPS samples for transition countries by sector and size in 2002 and 2005 is shown below.

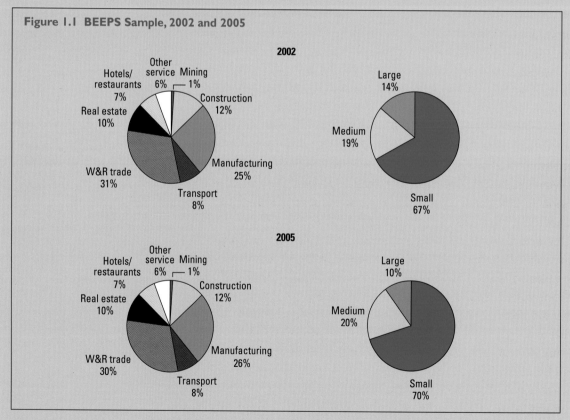

Figure 1.1 BEEPS Sample, 2002 and 2005

For more information and for access to the BEEPS data, see World Bank 2006a: www.worldbank.org/eca/econ or www.worldbank.org/eca/governance.

system gone and economic rules and social norms changing quickly, corruption also began to grow in the delivery of public services, such as health care and utilities, and in other public functions, such as licensing, inspections, and tax and customs administration.[1] As the role and importance of judicial systems changed with the emergence of the private economy, corruption also increased in the courts.[2] By the close of the first decade of transition, corruption was perceived throughout the region to be widespread and pernicious.

The growing citizen disenchantment motivated an increasing number of prominent political and civic leaders across the region. As Milos Zeman assumed his post as the Czech Republic's Prime Minister in 1998, he declared that "privatization as it was conducted in the Czech Republic over the last five years was corruption, nothing more. It created an environment in which the idea that you got something for nothing became the norm."[3] Slovak Deputy Prime Minister Ivan Miklos spearheaded a strong anticorruption program immediately upon taking office at the end of the Meciar regime in 1998, highlighting the abuses of the Meciar years and noting that "corruption is a problem in every country, but it is a bigger issue in transition countries like ours."[4] In Bulgaria a number of nongovernmental organizations (NGOs) came together in 1998 to launch *Coalition 2000*, an initiative designed to monitor and promote public awareness about what they saw as a growing problem of corruption in that country.[5]

More recently, two of the most notable political transitions in the region in 2003 and 2004—the "Rose Revolution" in Georgia that removed Eduard Shevardnadze from power and the "Orange Revolution" in Ukraine that ousted Leonid Kuchma—were both powered by citizen anger about corruption and bad government. Mikhail Saakashvili, who was elected to the Presidency in Georgia, declared immediately that rooting out rampant corruption would be his highest priority. Shortly after his election, Ukrainian President Yuschenko declared that "I know what responsibility these words carry, but I have the honor of telling you — my government will not steal."[6] The new Prime Minister of Albania, Sali Berisha, who took office in September 2005, similarly campaigned on a strong anticorruption platform and pledged that "uprooting corruption will be the first challenge for our new government. In Albania corruption has developed into a sophisticated system, with state capture, fiscal evasion and bribing at dramatic levels."[7] While not every leader who campaigns on an anticorruption platform necessarily follows through effectively if elected, strong and committed leadership can make a difference, as will be illustrated further in this report.

The international community also dramatically increased its attention to the issue of corruption during the 1990s. The political developments in transition economies gave this increased attention a strong push, as the breakup of the Soviet Union and resulting softening of superpower competition created conditions in which international organizations, donor agencies, and NGOs could be more forthright in challenging corrupt regimes in developing countries. The increasing attention grew in part out of a change in thinking in the economics profession, as a rapidly growing body of economic research in the early 1990s highlighted the importance of well-functioning institutions for economic growth and the harmful effects of corruption on development.[8] The World Bank adopted a formal anticorruption strategy in 1997,[9] and the amount of lending and analytic work devoted to understanding and tackling problems of corruption increased dramatically in the late 1990s, including in the ECA region.[10]

A wide variety of other international organizations and NGOs have also devoted extensive resources to the fight against corruption in transition countries. The European Union (EU), for example, has focused on anticorruption efforts in setting timetables for EU accession for new and prospective members.[11] The Organisation for Economic Co-operation and Development (OECD) has established an Anticorruption Network for Transition Economies.[12] The Stability Pact for southeastern Europe has established an Anticorruption Initiative (SPAI) to help coordinate anticorruption activities in the Balkans.[13] The Council of Europe has set up the Group of States Against Corruption (GRECO) to support peer monitoring of anticorruption initiatives among member countries.[14] Transparency International and other NGOs support research and monitoring and have a strong set of country-level affiliates who often spearhead discussions on governance and corruption issues.[15] In-depth analytic work also increased substantially in the 1990s and early 2000s, with academic and donor institutions supporting a variety of in-country and cross-country surveys to throw light on political and institutional realities in transition countries (see Box 1.2).

In sum, plenty of attention has been paid to the issue of corruption in transition economies—its causes, its costs to society, and how to reduce it. Is this attention making a difference? Is widespread corruption an endemic and long-term feature of these newly capitalist economies, or is

Box 1.2 How do the BEEPS results compare to other corruption indicators?

Indicators of corruption outcomes abound, although they vary by definition (firm-level bribery versus probability of losing investments), methodology (expert assessments by foreigners versus surveys of people in the country), and transparency of methodology. Aggregates of other indicators, such as the Transparency International Corruption Perceptions Index (TI-CPI), are popular among researchers because they cover hundreds of countries, and they have been useful for raising the profile of corruption and governance issues. They are not, however, designed for making comparisons over time, as they are rescaled each year and the implicit definition of what is being measured also changes over time. Nevertheless, the overall trends for the Europe and Central Asia region evident in some of the underlying indicators—including the firm-level surveys done by the World Economic Forum and the expert-opinion measures produced by Freedom House *Nations in Transit*—are consistent with the main conclusion emerging from the BEEPS: Firm-level corruption fell significantly between 2002 and 2005. For a fuller discussion of various governance indicators and their application in transition countries, see Knack (2006).

it a more transitory feature that will decline over time once market and institutional reforms take hold? Are transition countries really more corrupt than European countries further west? This report provides the latest evidence on these questions.

Notes

1. Between 1998 and 2002, the World Bank, often in cooperation with the United States Agency for International Development (USAID), carried out corruption diagnostic surveys of firms, citizens, and public officials in Albania, Bosnia and Herzegovina, Georgia, Latvia, the Kyrgyz Republic, Kazakhstan, Romania, and the Slovak Republic. Households commonly reported unofficial payments for health and educational services and to traffic police, while firms commonly reported bribing customs and tax officials, the courts, and police. Several of these countries are now leading reformers in the region and have made major strides in tackling corruption, as will be shown in this report. The country survey results can be found at World Bank 2006a: www.worldbank.org/eca/econ or www.worldbank.org/eca/governance.

2. Anderson, Bernstein, and Gray (2005) and Anderson and Gray (forthcoming).

3. Quoted in Hessel and Murphy (2004).

4. *The Times* (United Kingdom), February 21, 2001.

5. Coalition 2000 (2006).

6. Radio Free Europe/Radio Liberty Belarus and Ukraine Report. Vol. 7, No. 6, 11 February 2005

7. Speech to the diplomatic corps in Tirana, Oct. 17, 2005. http://www.keshilliministrave.al/english/lajm.asp?id=5481

8. See, for example, Bardhan (1997), North (1990), and World Bank (2002). For reviews of recent literature on corruption and development, see Lambsdorff (2005) and Svensson (2005).

9. World Bank (1997).

10. See World Bank 2006a: http://www.worldbank.org/eca/econ or http://www.worldbank.org/eca/governance for details of the Bank's anticorruption work in the ECA region.

11. EUMAP 2006: http://www.eumap.org.

12. OECD 2006: http://www.oecd.org.

13. Stability Pact Anticorruption Initiative 2006: http://www.spai-rslo.org.

14. Council of Europe Group of Countries Against Corruption 2006: http://www.greco.coe.int.

15. Transparency International 2006: http://www.transparency.org. Other prominent groups promoting good governance in ECA countries include the Open Society Institute (OSI), the National Democratic Institute (NDI), the Organization for Security and Co-operation in Europe (OSCE), the International Crisis Group, and Freedom House.

2

Patterns of Corruption, 2002–2005

A S NOTED IN CHAPTER 1, RHETORIC ABOUT CORRUPTION INCREAS-
ingly permeated political speech in the 1990s and early 2000s,
although reforms were often delivered with less vigor. But some
countries did take corruption seriously, and many transition leaders
undertook reforms to combat it. These reforms varied in their policy and
institutional arrangements, reflecting differing degrees of emphasis on
prevention and punishment. Have they been successful? This chapter
examines recent patterns and trends in broad indicators of corruption.
Chapter 3 explores factors that influenced the trends, including growth,
institutions, and politics, while Chapter 4 looks in more depth at sector-
specific policies and corruption outcomes.

The analysis in this chapter focuses on the period from 2002 through
2005, complementing the analysis of changes from 1999 to 2002
described in detail in ACT2. In both cases the analysis focuses on four
summary measures of corruption: (i) the extent to which firms see corruption as a problem for business; (ii) the frequency of bribery; (iii) the
amount of money paid in bribes (that is, the "bribe tax"); and (iv) the
impact of state capture on firms. The first summary measure is meant as
a composite, while the second and third focus on *administrative corruption* and the fourth on *state capture*. Administrative corruption refers to
bribery by individuals, groups, or firms in the private sector to influence
the *implementation* of laws and regulations, while state capture refers to
bribery to influence the *formulation* or *content* of laws and regulations.[1]
While somewhat different conceptually, both types of corruption can
have major impacts on the business environment. Administrative corrup-

tion tends to weaken the rule of law by undermining a government's ability to implement laws and regulations, while both administrative corruption and state capture can have pernicious effects on economic competition by restricting market entry and distributing economic preferences to influential elites.

Corruption as a problem for business

The first indicator of corruption measured by the BEEPS focuses on the bottom line for firms: How much of a problem is corruption for the operation and growth of firms, both in and of itself and compared with the many other problems firms face? Figure 2.1 shows the average percentage of firms that viewed corruption as a problem for the operation and growth of their business in 2002 and 2005, by country.[2] The arrows illustrate the direction and extent of change. The figure also shows analogous levels in 2005 for the six nontransition comparator countries—Ireland, Germany, Spain, Greece, Turkey and Portugal.[3]

Although there was generalized improvement across transition countries, some had remarkable improvement while others showed a

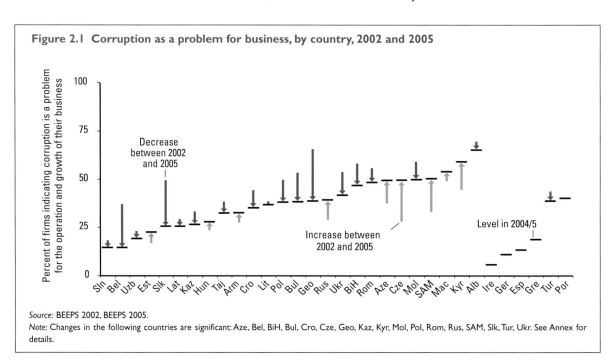

Figure 2.1 Corruption as a problem for business, by country, 2002 and 2005

Source: BEEPS 2002, BEEPS 2005.

Note: Changes in the following countries are significant: Aze, Bel, BiH, Bul, Cro, Cze, Geo, Kaz, Kyr, Mol, Pol, Rom, Rus, SAM, Slk, Tur, Ukr. See Annex for details.

worsening trend. Among the eight new EU members,[4] firms in the Slovak Republic reported the largest improvement and firms in Poland the second largest, while the Czech Republic was the only country in the group where significantly more firms reported corruption to be a problem in 2005 than three years earlier. Indeed, the Czech Republic is among the half-dozen transition countries where businesses perceive the most significant corruption problem. Changes in the other five new EU members between 2002 and 2005 were minor or insignificant.

In southeast Europe the findings are mixed. The good news is that the two countries that will soon join the EU, Bulgaria and Romania, both showed significant improvement, although levels are still high—in Romania about half of the firms in the survey indicated that corruption is a problem for the operation and growth of their business. Croatia's results were also better in 2005 than in 2002. However, the survey showed a worsening situation in Serbia and Montenegro, and the slight improvement in Bosnia and Herzegovina still leaves it at a high level (with nearly 50 percent of firms saying corruption is a problem), similar to Romania and Serbia and Montenegro. Albania remains the worst performer among all transition countries, that is, the country where the most firms (about two thirds) reported corruption to be a problem.

Findings are also mixed in the southern Commonwealth of Independent States (CIS). Firms in Georgia, and to a lesser extent Moldova, reported corruption to be much less of a problem, albeit from very high levels three years earlier, while firms in Azerbaijan and the Kyrgyz Republic reported a worsening of the problem. The findings for Armenia, Tajikistan, and Uzbekistan, which did not differ much between 2002 and 2005, indicate that firms in those countries do not view corruption as a problem to the same extent as elsewhere in the CIS. Among the northern CIS countries, all showed improvement except for Russia, which is now more or less on a par with Ukraine.[5]

Figure 2.2 shows the average values for 2005 by subregion and adds a measure of the relative value of firms' ratings on corruption compared to their ratings on the many other problems they face in the business environment. The relative assessments mirror the absolute assessments, with firms in southeast Europe and the southern CIS reporting corruption to be a worse problem on average than the many other problems they face, and firms in northern CIS and the EU-8 placing corruption on a par with other problems. Firms in the European comparator countries see corruption as a less serious problem than others they face.

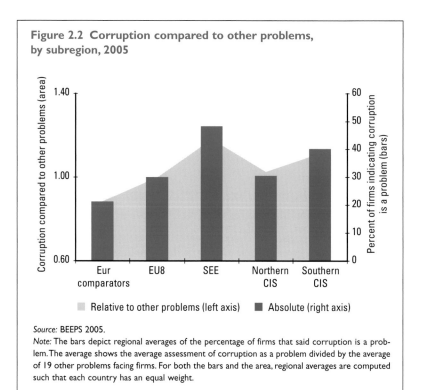

Figure 2.2 Corruption compared to other problems, by subregion, 2005

Source: BEEPS 2005.

Note: The bars depict regional averages of the percentage of firms that said corruption is a problem. The average shows the average assessment of corruption as a problem divided by the average of 19 other problems facing firms. For both the bars and the area, regional averages are computed such that each country has an equal weight.

Bribe frequency

The finding that many firms see corruption to be less of a problem for business in 2005 than three years earlier, both in absolute terms and relative to other problems, is welcome news. Yet corruption as a problem for business is the most subjective of the assessments covered by the BEEPS. It is possible, for example, that corruption is viewed as less of a problem simply because it has become commonplace and firms are now used to it.

In this section, we examine what firms are saying about the extent of firm-level bribery. Managers were asked to assess how frequently firms like theirs made unofficial payments to get things done.[6] The percent of firms responding in 2002 and 2005 that such payments were frequent is depicted in Figure 2.3. Transition countries as a whole showed a decline in the frequency of unofficial payments, with the strongest improvements in the new members of the European Union and the southern CIS. Among the new EU members, the Slovak Republic had the most notable

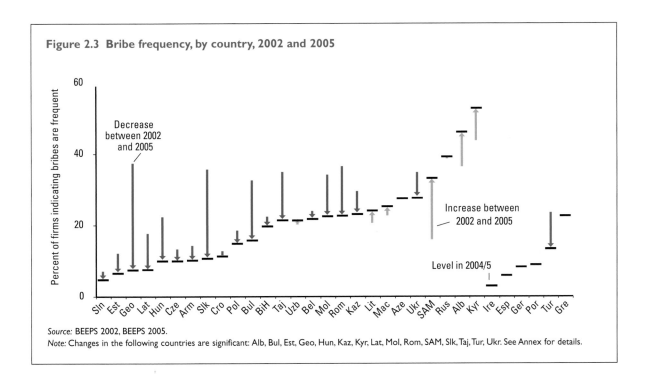

Figure 2.3 Bribe frequency, by country, 2002 and 2005

Source: BEEPS 2002, BEEPS 2005.
Note: Changes in the following countries are significant: Alb, Bul, Est, Geo, Hun, Kaz, Kyr, Lat, Mol, Rom, SAM, Slk, Taj, Tur, Ukr. See Annex for details.

improvement, while firms in Latvia and Estonia also reported that unofficial payments were less frequent than in 2002. The southern CIS saw improvements in Moldova, Tajikistan, and especially Georgia, all from relatively high figures in 2002. The country with the worst deterioration, and from an already high level, was the Kyrgyz Republic (see Box 2.1). In southeast Europe, more firms in both Albania and Serbia and Montenegro said unofficial payments were frequent in 2005 compared to three years earlier, while the reverse occurred—that is, the reported frequency of bribery fell markedly—in Bulgaria and Romania. In the northern CIS, Kazakhstan and Ukraine had modest but significant improvements, whereas no change was reported in Belarus or Russia.

Notwithstanding the trends, firms in many transition countries continue to report high frequency of unofficial payments. About one half of firms in the Kyrgyz Republic and Albania, and more than one quarter of firms in Russia, Serbia and Montenegro, Ukraine, and Azerbaijan, said that bribery was frequent. The least frequent bribery is reported in some of the western European comparators (Ireland and Spain, but not Greece, where bribe frequency appears quite high) as well as in Slovenia, Estonia, and Latvia. And the marked improvements in Georgia and the Slovak

Box 2.1 The Kyrgyz Republic—still a long way to go

The Kyrgyz Republic faces a big challenge in addressing the problem of administrative corruption. In 2005 it rated first among all countries surveyed by the BEEPS in the frequency of bribes, second (to Azerbaijan) in the level of the bribe tax, and second (to Albania) in the extent to which corruption is a problem for business. Moreover, two of the three indicators—the frequency of bribes and the extent to which firms see corruption as a problem for business—increased from 2002 to 2005, in contrast to the trends in most of the countries in the region. And these trends are occurring despite efforts at economic and institutional reforms since the early 1990s.

Numerous initiatives, focusing largely on legal frameworks, have been undertaken in recent years to deal with governance and corruption issues, included adoption of an anticorruption law, establishment of Councils on Good Governance (in 2003 and 2004) to advise on anticorruption policy, legal reform to improve the business environment, establishment of an anticorruption commission in 2005, a new civil service law to promote a professional civil service with merit-based appointments, a law on the declaration of income and assets of high state officials, and reforms to make public finances more transparent. However, there has been relatively little attention paid to implementation, capacity building, and upgrading of managerial skills.

Practical enforcement and implementation have been slow, and in practice, these actions have not yet had significant impact. For example, there have been no prosecutions under the anticorruption law, and the councils on good governance have had unclear and overlapping mandates. Action plans and anticorruption strategies have consisted mainly of lists of proposals to change the legal framework and carry out public information campaigns. The laws to improve the business environment have not been implemented, and the regime of multiple inspections of business activity remains essentially unchanged. On the positive side, the key provisions on competitive appointments in the Civil Service Law are beginning to be implemented in practice, and it is likely that the impact of these will be felt in coming years if the authorities fully commit to effective and consistent implementation. One small but important step forward has been the publication of income and asset declarations for high state officials, but even this will only improve governance to the extent that the authorities provide an environment to allow the media and civil society to hold officials accountable for the origins of their wealth.

These limited outcomes are the result of an unbalanced governance reform and anticorruption strategy. Reforms, many of them supported by the World Bank and other donors, have focused on introducing legislative changes with inadequate attention paid to implementation and enforcement. The Kyrgyz Republic had a revolution at the time of the survey, and so the results largely reflect developments under the previous administration. The next survey will shed light on the new government's ability and willingness to start to deal with corruption by reducing opportunities for rent seeking and changing public perceptions about what is tolerated in society. The former requires regulatory reform to improve the business environment and promote competition in the economy, stronger emphasis on transparency in government, a movement from patronage to meritocracy in the public service, and a wider distribution of both power and accountability through decentralization and other means. The latter requires strong and consistent leadership, outreach, and results.

Republic have brought them to levels similar to the best performers in the region in 2005.

Figure 2.4 shows the converse of Figure 2.3—the percentage of all firms that asserted that unofficial payments are *never* paid by firms like theirs to get things done. Results are grouped by subregion. The same improvements emerge, but only in the European comparators do more than half the firms assert that unofficial payments are never required to get things done.

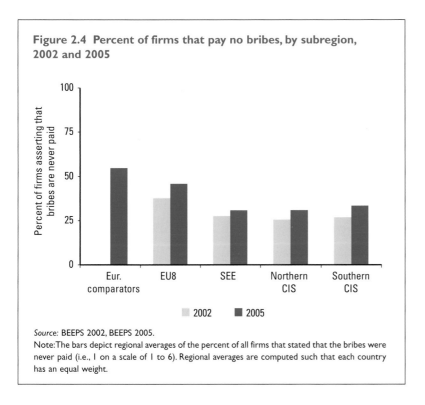

Figure 2.4 Percent of firms that pay no bribes, by subregion, 2002 and 2005

Source: BEEPS 2002, BEEPS 2005.
Note: The bars depict regional averages of the percent of all firms that stated that the bribes were never paid (i.e., 1 on a scale of 1 to 6). Regional averages are computed such that each country has an equal weight.

The overall trends in both the frequency of firm-level bribery and the assessments of corruption as a problem for doing business both point generally in the same promising direction. Concerns that corruption has become so commonplace that firms now accept it therefore might not be warranted. However, digging deeper into the firm-level responses to these two survey questions reveals some interesting patterns. The two combinations of answers that show nontolerance of corruption by society are (i) a no on both questions—bribes are not frequent and corruption is not a problem for business—and (ii) a yes on both questions—bribes are frequent and corruption is a problem.[7] As seen in Figure 2.5 and Figure 2.6, over 80 percent of firms in the European comparator countries answered one of these two ways in 2005, compared to about 60–70 percent in the transition countries.

The other two combinations of answers are more problematic. For example, a relatively high percentage of firms in southeast Europe—about one third—viewed corruption as a problem for business even though they reported that bribery was not frequent (Figure 2.7). This could reflect a concern with types of corruption that do not necessarily

Figure 2.5 Frequent and a problem, by subregion, 2002 and 2005

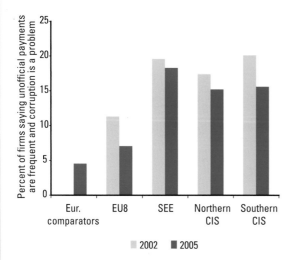

Figure 2.6 Not a problem and not frequent, by subregion, 2002 and 2005

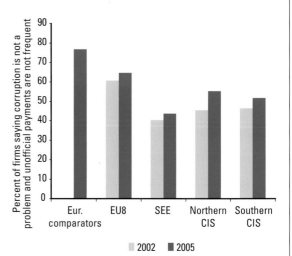

Figure 2.7 Problem but not frequent, by subregion, 2002 and 2005

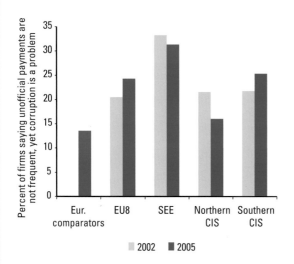

Figure 2.8 Frequent but not a problem, by subregion, 2002 and 2005

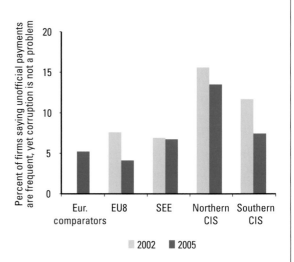

Source: BEEPS 2002, BEEPS 2005.

Note: Regional averages are computed such that each country has an equal weight.

involve bribes, such as theft of state resources or state capture by narrow economic interests. In contrast, a relatively high percentage of northern CIS firms—about one out of eight (and one out of five in Russia)—reported that firms frequently make unofficial payments to get things done, yet corruption is not an obstacle to their business (Figure 2.8). These firms, arguably, find bribery acceptable. A positive finding from the 2005 BEEPS is that such "acceptance" is not only very low in absolute terms (less than 5 percent of firms in the new EU members and European comparators and less than 10 percent in southeast Europe and the southern CIS) but also appears to be falling in every subregion, with the exception of southeast Europe.

The bribe tax

The third summary measure of corruption tracked by BEEPS is the "bribe tax," which is the percentage of annual firm revenue paid in bribes, as reported by the firms themselves. The bribe tax is complementary to bribe frequency as an indicator, and the two do not necessarily move together. In some countries with high levels of "petty" corruption, bribe frequency may be high while the overall bribe tax is not particularly onerous. In contrast, where avenues for corruption are tightly controlled within a government bureaucracy, firms may face high bribe taxes on selected transactions but relatively infrequent requests for bribes on a day-to-day basis.

Across all of the transition countries, the average percent of revenues paid in bribes (weighing each country's result equally) declined from 1.6 percent in 2002 to 1.1 percent in 2005. Many firms in every country said zero, and these responses are included in these averages. Among firms with nonzero responses—that is, firms that admit to making unofficial payments—the bribe tax declined from 3.6 percent to 2.9 percent of revenues. Major improvement is evident in most countries, but the levels remain substantially higher than in the European comparators (Figure 2.9). Large declines in the bribe tax occurred in Georgia and Tajikistan, as well as five of the six countries in southeast Europe. Two of these six (Albania and Serbia and Montenegro, as well as the Kyrgyz Republic in the CIS) had improvements in the bribe tax even while bribe frequency was increasing, an indication that petty corruption was expanding but the overall cost to firms (as a share of revenues) was not. Romania showed a

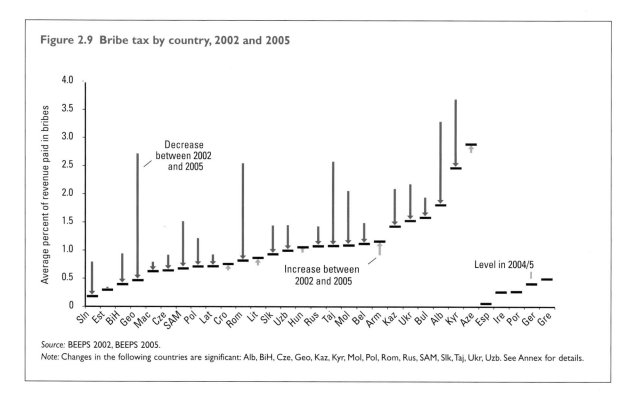

Figure 2.9 Bribe tax by country, 2002 and 2005

Source: BEEPS 2002, BEEPS 2005.

Note: Changes in the following countries are significant: Alb, BiH, Cze, Geo, Kaz, Kyr, Mol, Pol, Rom, Rus, SAM, Slk, Taj, Ukr, Uzb. See Annex for details.

huge decline in the bribe tax, matching its improvement on the other two corruption indicators discussed earlier. Half of the EU-8 showed reductions in the bribe tax, most notably in Slovenia. The bribe tax fell even in the Czech Republic, where firms reported no change in bribe frequency and an increase in corruption as a problem doing business. Among European comparators, the bribe tax is the highest in Greece and the eastern part of Germany.

While the results regarding the bribe tax are encouraging, with 16 out of 26 transition countries showing significant reductions and none showing a significant increase, two important facts should be kept in mind. First, the levels of the bribe tax remain quite high, with only Estonia and Slovenia matching the average for the European comparators. Average firm-level net profits were 12 percent of gross revenues, meaning that a 1 percent bribe tax would be equivalent to about 8 percent of net profits. Second, *declines in the average bribe tax do not necessarily mean that the absolute amount paid in bribes has fallen,* since the bribe tax is measured as a share of firm-level revenues. The size of the economy in every transition country has grown rapidly over the past three years, by an average of

63 percent in nominal terms, and the amount of money changing hands in unofficial payments could well have increased even as the share of bribes in total revenues fell. Indeed, if firms' revenues grew at the same rate as GDP, the average responses to the bribe tax question imply that the total amount of money paid in bribes increased in most countries. In Croatia, Lithuania, Armenia, and Hungary, for example, despite the fact that there was no significant change in the level of the bribe tax as a share of revenues, the rapid growth in these economies implies that the total volume of bribery increased substantially from 2002 to 2005.

State capture

The fourth summary measure of corruption tracked by BEEPS is the impact of state capture on individual firms. As noted earlier, state capture refers to corruption in the law-making process. State capture can be extremely pernicious to an economy and society, because it can fundamentally and permanently distort the "rules of the game" in favor of a few privileged insiders. Although the concept is easy to grasp, it is very difficult to measure. BEEPS makes an attempt by asking respondents to what extent the provision of unofficial payments, gifts, or other benefits to parliamentarians to affect their votes or to government officials to affect the content of government decrees had a *direct* impact on the respondent's business.[8] Note that the question does not ask whether the firm *made* such payments, but whether such payments by others affected the firm directly.

Figure 2.10 shows the change in perceptions of the impact of state capture from 2002 to 2005, measured as the average of the scores on the two dimensions (payments to parliamentarians and to government officials). The highest levels of state capture are perceived by firms in southeast Europe—Bosnia and Herzegovina, Albania, FYR Macedonia, and Serbia and Montenegro. Major improvements from 2002 and 2005 were reported in Bulgaria, Latvia, the Slovak Republic, Ukraine, Georgia, and Slovenia, and the 2005 results were significantly worse than in 2002 in Albania, Armenia, Russia, and Azerbaijan. The reasons for Georgia's notable improvement on this and other measures of corruption[9] are addressed further in Box 2.2. As discussed in the next chapter, the results for Uzbekistan and Belarus have a somewhat different interpretation given these countries' slow progress in transition.

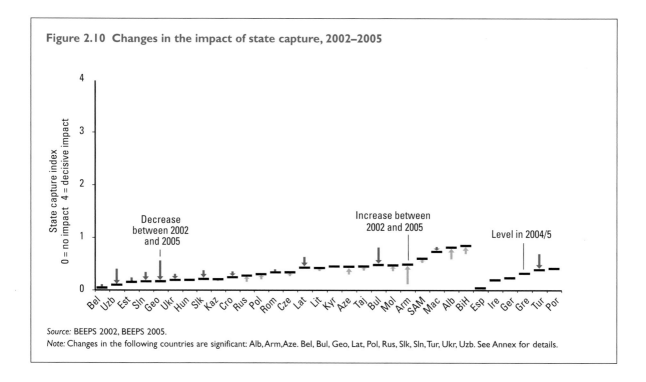

Figure 2.10 Changes in the impact of state capture, 2002–2005

Source: BEEPS 2002, BEEPS 2005.

Note: Changes in the following countries are significant: Alb, Arm, Aze. Bel, Bul, Geo, Lat, Pol, Rus, Slk, Sln, Tur, Ukr, Uzb. See Annex for details.

As with other measures of corruption, the impact of state capture is perceived by firms to be somewhat lower in several European comparators—Germany, Ireland, and Spain—but relatively high in Portugal and Turkey and at about the average for transition countries in Greece. Of all of the measures of corruption presented in this chapter, this one shows the least difference between transition and comparator countries. The recent lobbying scandals in many OECD countries underscore the fact that state capture is a persistent problem even in the most advanced economies.

Summary

This chapter has summarized the BEEPS results for the transition countries and European comparators along four broad measures of corruption: the extent to which firms consider corruption a problem for business, the frequency of bribery, the amount of bribes paid (as a share of revenues), and the extent to which state capture affects firms. Considering all of the results from both the full BEEPS sample and a smaller

Box 2.2 Georgia —strong leadership yields results

Prior rounds of the BEEPS highlighted that firms in Georgia perceived very high levels of corruption. This changed dramatically with the 2005 round of the survey. The largest reductions in corruption among all transition countries from 2002 and 2005 occurred in Georgia. Firms report that both administrative corruption and state capture have fallen markedly and that corruption is far less of a problem to business. These results are not surprising to those who know the country well, as the pace of economic and institutional reform in Georgia since the "Rose Revolution" in November 2003 has been impressive. For the past two years policy making has been led by a cadre of leaders who gained power on an anticorruption platform and placed governance at the top of the reform agenda.

The leadership has taken bold actions to fight corruption, reduce the burden of the state in the economy, and develop a fiscally sustainable social safety net. As a result they have, in a very short period of time, reformed corrupt institutions and changed public perceptions along many fronts. The executive branch has been reorganized and streamlined and has introduced a cabinet style of government. The government has greatly simplified the regulatory framework for the business sector, implemented a major tax reform, improved management of public finances through adoption of a medium-term expenditure framework (MTEF) and single treasury account for central government, and strengthened oversight institutions. The Chamber of Control of Georgia reopened and resumed its auditing functions in 2005, and in 2006 the government submitted a law to parliament to empower the Chamber of Control as supreme auditing institution. In addition to these institutional reforms, a substantial share of the police force (including the entire traffic police) and a large number of tax and customs officials have been dismissed. Furthermore, higher salaries and stricter rules for hiring and firing in these agencies have created an incentive system that reinforces professional behavior and discourages corruption. These and many other actions of the new government have reduced opportunities for bribery and are changing the public's expectations about the extent to which corruption will be tolerated.

Many of these changes have been accomplished by a relatively small group of young and very determined reformers. Over the next few years, the government needs to translate these impressive gains into lasting institutional change. This will require decisive reforms to strengthen the rule of law. Restructuring the legal and judicial system, ensuring and safeguarding its professional competency, and strengthening its independence are at the core of these reforms. Similarly, to institutionalize the reforms of the state, Georgia will need to build a more efficient and accountable public administration by modernizing the rules for hiring, firing, monitoring, and evaluating public employees and for determining the salaries they receive. Equally important is supporting the development of robust mechanisms for feedback from civil society. In the long term an informed public and civil society, an independent media, and tolerance of constructive criticism of the leadership are essential to sustaining the gains from reform. Committed leadership is important, but transparent, accountable, and well-functioning institutions are the key to good governance over the long term.

"panel" of selected firms interviewed in both 2002 and 2005 (see Box 2.3), there appears to be a broad consensus that corruption has declined markedly dramatically over the past three years in Georgia and the Slovak Republic, and to a somewhat lesser extent in Poland and Latvia. The results also point to improvements in Bulgaria and Romania, which bodes well for their entry into the European Union, and to significant improvements along some dimensions (albeit from relatively high levels) in Ukraine, Moldova, Kazakhstan, and Tajikistan.

Results are more mixed for other transition countries. Rapid economic growth has helped to dampen the burden of the bribe tax almost everywhere, but the frequency of bribery and the perceived problems

Box 2.3 Do panel data show the same results as the full BEEPS sample?

Some of the firms interviewed for the BEEPS in 2002 were interviewed again in 2005, and the BEEPS data from this "panel" of firms expands the range of analysis that can be done with the survey data. Because the same firms were interviewed each year, the differences in their responses from 2002 to 2005 are less likely to reflect idiosyncrasies of the firms and more likely to reflect the changes in the business environment during that period. There are also limitations to this panel data, however, most notably the relatively small size of the sample in each country.

It is interesting nonetheless to compare the results from the broad firm sample (as discussed throughout this report) and the panel on three broad corruption indicators—corruption as a problem for business, bribe frequency, and bribe tax.

Figure 2.11 shows the percentage of firms in the panel for each country that reported corruption either improving, staying the same, or worsening between 2002 and 2005. (Only countries with significant changes are included.) In most cases the results are similar to those coming out of the full BEEPS survey. With regard to corruption as a problem doing business, large improvements were reported by both the panel and the larger BEEPS sample in Belarus, Bulgaria, Croatia, Georgia, and the Slovak Republic. In contrast, both the panel and the larger sample reported corruption to be a worse problem in 2005 than in 2002 in Armenia and FYR Macedonia. With regard to bribe frequency, improvements were reported by both the panel and the larger sample in Bulgaria, Georgia, Kazakhstan, Latvia, Romania, and the Slovak Republic. Finally, the findings on bribe tax were consistent in finding improvements in a large number of countries. Across all three measures, there was not a single case where a statistically significant trend apparent from the overall sample was contradicted by a significant trend in the other direction in the panel sample.

Figure 2.11 Changes in corruption according to panel data

Corruption as a problem doing business 2002 and 2005

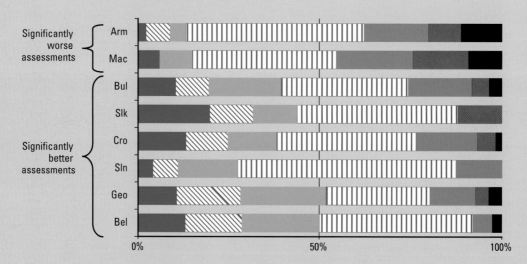

Bribe frequency 2002 and 2005

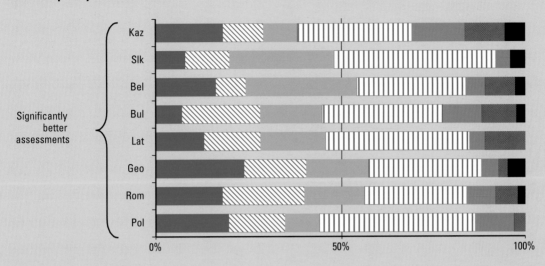

Bribe tax 2002 and 2005

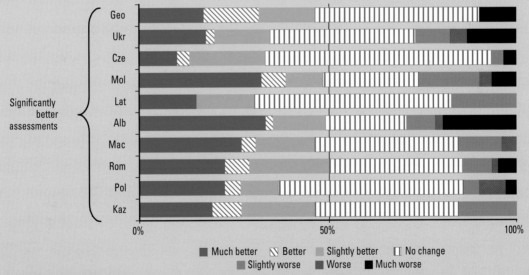

Source: BEEPS 2002, BEEPS 2005.

Note: For the chart on corruption as a problem, "slightly better" means that corruption as a problem doing business improved by 1 point on a 4-point scale; "better" means a 2-point improvement; "much better" means an improvement of 3 points. For the chart on bribe frequency, "slightly better" means that reported bribe frequency improved by 1 point on a 6-point scale; "better" means a 2-point improvement; "much better" means an improvement of 3, 4, or 5 points. For the chart on the bribe tax, "slightly better" means that reported bribe tax was between 0 and 1% smaller in 2005 than in 2002; "better" 1 to 2%; "much better" 2 or more percent. For all three charts the "worse" measures are constructed in an analogous way. Countries with fewer than 20 panel observations were not included in these charts. Statistical significance refers to the 10% level for a *t*-test of whether the mean equals zero.

caused by corruption for businesses have not changed markedly in most countries and have increased in a few. According to firms, Albania and the Kyrgyz Republic continue, as in 2002, to have the worst corruption indicators of all 33 countries surveyed, and some indicators in Azerbaijan, Russia, and Serbia and Montenegro appear to have worsened from 2002 to 2005. Furthermore, firms in most transition countries—other than perhaps Estonia and Slovenia—still report significantly higher levels of corruption than Western European comparators—most notably Ireland, Spain, and Germany, as some indicators in Greece, Portugal, and Turkey are not too different than those in the transition countries.

Notes

1. These concepts were introduced in ACT1 and discussed further in ACT2.

2. Figure 2.1 shows the percentage of firms responding that corruption is a moderate or major obstacle (see methodological annex).

3. Two other comparator countries, the Republic of Korea and Vietnam, were also surveyed. As most of the transition countries look westward for models, this report focuses on the European comparators. Responses of Korean firms were generally in step with those of the European comparators, while those of Vietnam resembled those of transition countries. Tables including these two countries were presented in EBRD (2005).

4. For ease of presentation, this report will use the following subregional groupings: The southern Commonwealth of Independent States (CIS) includes Armenia, Azerbaijan, Georgia, the Kyrgyz Republic, Moldova, Tajikistan, and Uzbekistan; The northern CIS includes Belarus, Kazakhstan, Russia, and Ukraine; Southeast Europe includes Albania, Bosnia and Herzegovina, Bulgaria, Croatia, FYR Macedonia, Romania, and Serbia and Montenegro; The EU-8 includes the Czech Republic, Estonia, Hungary, Latvia, Lithuania, Poland, the Slovak Republic, and Slovenia; The European Comparators include Germany, Greece, Ireland, Portugal, Spain, and Turkey. Chapter 4 will discuss how homogeneous these groups are with respect to survey responses on corruption.

5. The 2005 BEEPS findings for Belarus are in general very positive compared to the 2002 findings. Given the tight controls imposed by the Belarus government and the very limited scope for private activity in the economy, it is not clear to what extent these findings are comparable to those elsewhere in the region. The same is true for Uzbekistan. Chapter 3 discusses this issue in greater detail.

6. Figure 2.1 shows the percentage of firms responding that bribes were paid frequently, usually, or always (see Methodological Annex).

7. We are using the terms yes and no for ease of exposition. The questions were not yes/no questions; rather they were scaled response questions for which dummy variables were created by dividing the scales down the middle.

8. More dimensions of state capture, including payments to courts, central banks, and political parties, were included in the question in the 2002 BEEPS. Payment to parliamentarians and government officials were considered the essence of state capture, however, and thus the 2005 question was limited to these two. The differences between the average 2002 answers on the two dimensions versus all six dimensions, as reported in *Anticorruption in Transition 2* (World Bank 2004), were small—the two had a correlation of 0.93.

9. The general population also seems to note progress in Georgia. Transparency International's "Global Corruption Barometer" showed a marked reduction in perceptions of the prevalence of corruption in police, health, and education between 2004 and 2005, and in the 2005 survey of 500 urban respondents, 46 percent said corruption had declined compared to 20 percent that said corruption had increased (Transparency International 2004, 2005).

3

What Influences the Extent of Corruption?

AS DESCRIBED IN CHAPTER 2, FIRMS IN MANY TRANSITION COUNTRIES are reporting bribes to be less frequent and less costly, and corruption to be a smaller problem for business in 2005 as compared to three years earlier. Chapter 4 will examine in more detail how the levels and trends evident in the surveys relate to specific aspects of policy, but before doing so it is useful to step back at look at the bigger picture. In this chapter we examine how firm characteristics and certain broad aspects of the country environment (growth, institutions, and politics) affect the incidence of bribery.[1]

An integrated approach to examining firm- and country-specific factors in tandem was developed in *Anticorruption in Transition 2*.[2] That analysis found that the policy and institutional environment and certain firm-level characteristics both influenced the level of corruption, but a country's economic growth rate and certain political variables did not seem to have a statistically significant impact. Results of similar analysis using the 2005 BEEPS and additional findings from the panel data—available for the first time in 2005—are summarized below. The chapter then discusses the impact of slow reform and concentrated power in countries such as Belarus and Uzbekistan.

Firm characteristics

As in 2002, firm-level characteristics appear to play a strong role in determining who paid bribes and how much they pay. The playing field is rarely level even within a particular country, and different types of firms can face very different incentives and barriers to business. The 2005 BEEPS data reinforce the 2002 findings that, on average:

- private firms pay more bribes (as a share of revenues), pay them more frequently, and view corruption as a bigger problem for their business than do state-owned firms;
- manufacturing firms pay more bribes and pay them more frequently than firms in other sectors;
- firms in urban areas pay more bribes and pay them more frequently than firms in small towns or rural areas;
- small firms pay more bribes as a share of revenues than large firms (but feel less affected by state capture);
- foreign firms pay fewer bribes as a share of revenues than domestically owned firms; and
- firms pay fewer bribes the longer they have been in business.

Administrative corruption appears to have the greatest impact on new, small, private, domestically-owned firms in urban areas Figure 3.1.[3] Bribe frequency tends to be lower in comparator countries, for both new small firms and older larger firms.[4] More important, most of the "catching up" that has taken place is associated with a decreased bribe frequency for older, larger firms, not those most beset by bribery, the younger, newer firms. Corruption is clearly a barrier to entry for new private firms and a significant tax on private firms that manage to survive in the market. This result is highly problematic given the importance of private-sector development for a country's long-term economic growth.

The patterns that hold for the region, however, do not hold in every country. In some countries one effect dominates (for example, private ownership for Azerbaijan, location in cities for Hungary), and in others there is no strong firm-level pattern at all (for example, Bosnia and Herzegovina and Croatia). In the Czech Republic, firms in cities reported less frequent bribes than firms in smaller towns, and firms in cities viewed corruption as less of a problem for business in both the Czech Republic and Estonia. In Latvia older firms reported more frequent bribery, and in Russia, Moldova, and Estonia, small firms viewed corruption as less of a problem for business than larger firms. Country-specific analysis is clearly critical for the design of anticorruption strategies.

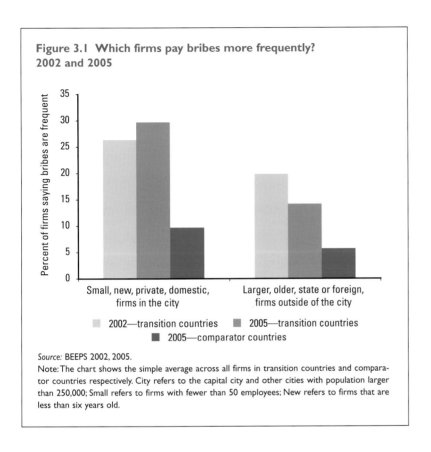

**Figure 3.1 Which firms pay bribes more frequently?
2002 and 2005**

Percent of firms saying bribes are frequent

Small, new, private, domestic,
firms in the city

Larger, older, state or foreign,
firms outside of the city

2002—transition countries   2005—transition countries
2005—comparator countries

Source: BEEPS 2002, 2005.
Note: The chart shows the simple average across all firms in transition countries and comparator countries respectively. City refers to the capital city and other cities with population larger
than 250,000; Small refers to firms with fewer than 50 employees; New refers to firms that are
less than six years old.

Economic growth

It is well-known that richer countries have lower levels of corruption, on
average, both across the world[5] and within Europe and Central Asia. The
relationship between corruption (as measured by bribe frequency) and
per capita GDP in the transition and comparator countries in 2005 is
shown in Figure 3.2. Economic literature on corruption suggests that the
causation runs both ways.[6] On the one hand, corruption hampers growth
by reducing the efficiency of public spending, the effectiveness of public
service delivery, and the attractiveness of the investment climate.
Moreover, corruption may lead to a misallocation of resources away
from more productive investments and toward more easily corruptible
projects. On the other hand, poorer countries have a harder time tackling
corruption, both because bribes may be more tempting when public
sector salaries are low and because it takes resources to fund "watchdog"
groups needed to prevent corruption, such as the press, accounting and

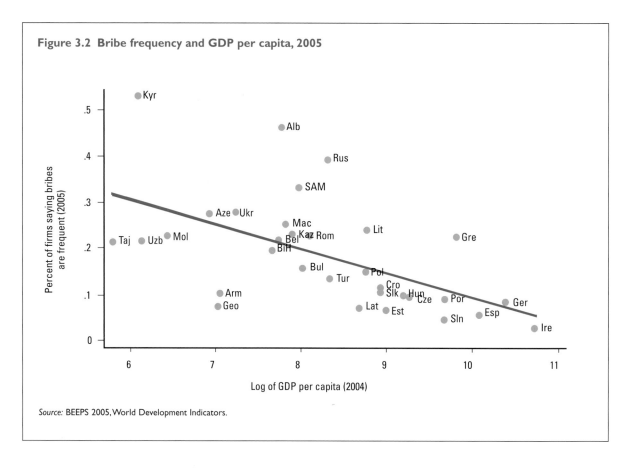

Figure 3.2 Bribe frequency and GDP per capita, 2005

Source: BEEPS 2005, World Development Indicators.

auditing services, and police and other investigative and law enforcement agencies. Confounding the relationship even further, other factors such as the institutional legacy inherited from colonial powers or social and cultural norms may affect both growth and levels of corruption.

Although this broad correlation between the levels of corruption and income is well-known, it is less clear whether rapid economic growth is associated with changes in corruption in the short-run. ACT2, drawing on the 2002 BEEPS data, did not find a significant cross-country correlation between recent rates of economic growth and the extent of corruption reported by firms. However, this correlation could be tested only at the country level in 2002, while the existence of the panel data set in the 2005 BEEPS allows us to go one step further to compare the changes in corruption indicators from 2002 to 2005 *as reported by individual firms* with average economic growth rates by country. The 2002–2005 average rate of GDP growth appears to have a significant positive relationship, other things being equal, with the change from 2002 to 2005 in the extent of payments to influence lawmaking (a form of state capture behavior). No such relationship is evident between aggregate growth and changes in the bribe tax or bribe frequency.

These results suggest that faster economic growth may exacerbate state capture in the short run even if it does not affect the overall level of administrative corruption. Such results are perhaps not surprising considering the corruption scandals that surround the political process even in the most advanced countries, where day-to-day administrative corruption is relatively rare. State capture is closely embedded in political processes and often benefits those at the highest levels of the social and political hierarchy. As such it may be harder to abate than administrative corruption, whose benefits more often accrue to "the little guy." Over the long term state capture does appear to fall as countries get richer (Figure 3.3), but it may take longer to reach that goal.

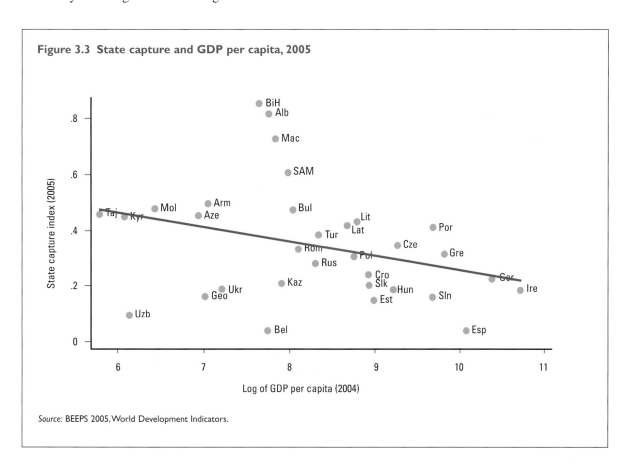

Figure 3.3 State capture and GDP per capita, 2005

Source: BEEPS 2005, World Development Indicators.

It is also interesting to explore the reverse hypothesis, that is, whether the levels of corruption in 2002 affected economic growth in subsequent years. Indeed, there is a significant positive correlation between the levels of both the bribe tax and the frequency of bribery in 2002 and the rates of GDP growth in 2003 and 2004. However, this correlation between corruption and growth rates disappears if an additional variable is introduced: natural resource (that is, fuel, oil, and minerals) exports as a share of GDP. The latter is itself positively correlated with levels of corruption, supporting the widely held view that natural-resource-exporting countries tend on average to have higher levels of corruption than countries with a more diversified export base.[7] The rapid rise in energy and mineral prices in the 2003–2005 period boosted growth rates in natural resource exporters. Levels of corruption in 2002 were not significantly correlated with economic growth rates from 2003 to 2004 after accounting for this phenomenon.

Policies and institutions

The view that better policies and institutions help to reduce the level of corruption is strongly supported by the 2005 data, confirming a key result of ACT2. We measure the quality of policies and institutions using the World Bank's 2004 Country Policy and Institutional Assessment (CPIA).[8] Analysis of the 2005 BEEPS data confirm the earlier finding that the frequency of bribery is strongly and negatively correlated with the overall quality of a country's economic policies and institutions for policy making and accountability. Committed leaders can make a real difference by promoting a variety of economic and institutional reforms, including tighter and more efficient fiscal policies, trade liberalization, stronger tax and customs administration, civil service reform to reduce patronage and reinforce meritocracy, and more effective and accountable judicial systems to discipline the behavior of elites (as discussed further in Chapter 4).

Following the scheme of analysis used in ACT2, the impact of political contestability was tested using (i) the length of time that a country's leadership has been in power and (ii) the existence of a parliamentary election in the most recent year before the survey. The first variable was not significantly related to the BEEPS measures of corruption, indicating that the tenure of a country's leaders does not, in and of itself, have a strong effect on the extent of firm-level corruption in the country. The second variable was statistically significant, however, indicating that bribery is more frequent around the time of a parliamentary election— not a surprising result given the likely financing needs of political parties and the uncertainties and short time horizons that tend to surround elections.

Slow progress in transition

The analysis in Chapter 2 highlighted the encouraging news that broad measures of corruption in the interactions between enterprises and the state have eased in many transition countries. This chapter has shown that a country's policies and institutions matter, and the decline in corruption is at least partially due to the considerable efforts that have been made over the past decade (as discussed further in the next chapter) to strengthen institutions of transparency and accountability and to improve the environment for doing business. While it is clear that adopting better policies and enacting institutional reforms can help reduce corruption, it is less clear how to spark such reforms in the first place, especially since there are often vested interests standing in the way of reform.

This question is motivated in part by a persistent feature of corruption surveys—that certain countries appear better in corruption surveys than most people expect. If one compares the BEEPS results with the results of surveys of "experts" (which tend to reflect general public attitudes more closely), such as those done by Freedom House, one finds significant discrepancies for certain countries. While the BEEPS measures of bribe frequency and bribe tax are highly correlated with the Freedom House indicator of corruption, the more overarching BEEPS assessment of corruption as a problem for doing business is not as strongly correlated.[9] The two countries with the largest deviations are Uzbekistan and Belarus, both former Soviet states for which the assessments of foreign experts are considerably worse than those of firms in the BEEPS. These are also generally considered to be two of the countries in the region with the least progress in transition.[10] A common reaction to this finding is to suspect that the survey data are affected by the political atmosphere in these countries. It is often argued, for example, that respondents may be afraid and thus less than forthcoming when providing responses to surveys that suggest that they may be involved in, or know about, corruption.

Although the hesitancy of respondents to provide accurate information may indeed affect survey results, there are also other possible explanations for the deviations between survey- and expert-based assessments. First, both may be right, with the divergence simply reflecting differences in the types of corruption being measured. Autocratic leaders are typically sustained through a type of implicit corruption, as resources of the state are diverted to support the power and lifestyle of the leader and those who help sustain his or her power. This need not translate, however, into corruption in routine interactions between firms and the state. Second, the survey responses may be more accurate than the experts' perceptions with regard to firm-level bribery. If a firm is reluctant to tell a stranger that "firms like mine" sometimes pay bribes because of fear of adverse consequences, they may also be reluctant to pay the bribes in the first place, an action for which there may be even worse consequences. The same logic applies from the official's perspective. In a more controlled environment an official (say an inspector) may be less likely to seek or accept bribes.

Finally, it is possible that the experts are right, but that firms in authoritarian regimes may not interpret routine bribery as corruption to the same extent as firms in more open and competitive economic systems. If an inspector's actions in demanding bribes are part of a systematic corruption network, approved and sanctioned from above, then the inspector will be less concerned with the consequences and may not see the behavior as wrong. Similarly, firms may view bribes as routine and hardly distinguishable from official payments for public services.

The BEEPS data provide some reassurance that most firms in all countries where BEEPS was carried out, including Belarus[11] and Uzbekistan, were in fact willing to talk about corruption, even if underreporting remains an issue. If firms in some countries were simply unwilling to talk about corruption, it seems logical that they would give favorable responses for all corruption questions. Yet among questions that ask about bribery by "firms like yours" (such as the bribe tax and each of the sector-specific bribe frequencies), 63 percent and 66 percent of firms in Belarus and Uzbekistan, respectively, gave a nonzero response to at least one of these questions. Among all questions involving corruption, including the above questions as well as the overall bribe frequency and the extent to which corruption is a problem for business, 97 percent and 91 percent of firms in Belarus and Uzbekistan, respectively, gave a nonzero response to at least one of the corruption questions. The overwhelming majority of firms in the sample in all countries did not categorically assert that they have no knowledge of or about corruption.

As noted at the beginning of this section, the findings of apparently low levels of firm-level bribery in countries with fewer civil liberties are not new. *Anticorruption in Transition—A Contribution to the Policy Debate* (World Bank 2000) remarked on Belarus' and Uzbekistan's low levels of corruption indicated by the first (1999) round of the BEEPS. The argument was based on the small size of the private sectors in these countries and the limited capacity that the private sector would have to capture the state. Generalizing beyond Belarus and Uzbekistan, the same report[12] presented an inverted-U relationship between state capture and civil liberties, arguing that other models of capture, such as political leaders capturing the state, may be present but not captured in the data.[13]

Empirical tests lend support to these conjectures. Using two different measures of the concentration of power, the stylized inverted-U relationship between concentrations of power and corruption come through clearly in the data from the 2005 round of the BEEPS. One indicator of the degree to which leaders may be willing to tolerate dissent is the existence, relative strength, and independence of civil society. The first measure of concentration of power, therefore, is the Freedom House *Nations in Transit* assessment of civil society.[14] Although the linear relationship between this variable and corruption (as indicated by BEEPS assessments of corruption as a problem doing business) is not significantly different from zero, an inverted-U pattern is highly significant,[15] as is clear from Figure 3.4 below. (The patterns are similar, but statistically weaker, for bribe tax and bribe frequency, an issue that will be discussed later in this section.) Moreover, the pattern is virtually unaffected when Belarus and Uzbekistan are dropped—they fit the pattern, but they are not driving it.[16]

A second measure of the concentration of political power is based on the Polity IV dataset's evaluation of executive restraints,[17] measuring the extent of institutionalized constraints on the decision-making powers of chief executives, whether individuals or collectivities. Again, the relationship is a significant one, also tracing the pattern of an inverted U (Figure 3.5). As the Polity assessments are also available for the comparator countries, the number of observations is somewhat larger than for the Freedom House measure, which is available only for transition countries.

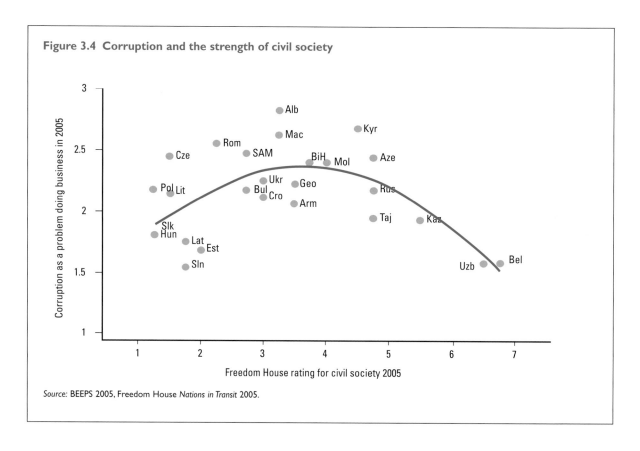

Figure 3.4 Corruption and the strength of civil society

Source: BEEPS 2005, Freedom House *Nations in Transit* 2005.

Although the inverted-U pattern in the relationship between the concentration of power and corruption as a problem doing business is very strong and robust, there is no such pattern evident in our other measures of corruption, the bribe tax and bribe frequency. Indeed, this may help explain an important interregional difference in the pattern of corruption. While the overall percentage of firms in Belarus and Uzbekistan report relatively low levels of corruption, these two countries, together with Russia and Kazakhstan, are among those where firms were most likely to report that unofficial payments are frequent, while simultaneously reporting that corruption is not a problem doing business. This is consistent with the conjecture stated at the outset of this section: In autocratic societies, where unofficial payments may be so systematized as to be indistinguishable from official payments (from a practical perspective), the understanding by firms of whether corruption is posing a problem could deviate substantially from the understanding of foreign observers.[18] The BEEPS provides some guidance on this issue as well.

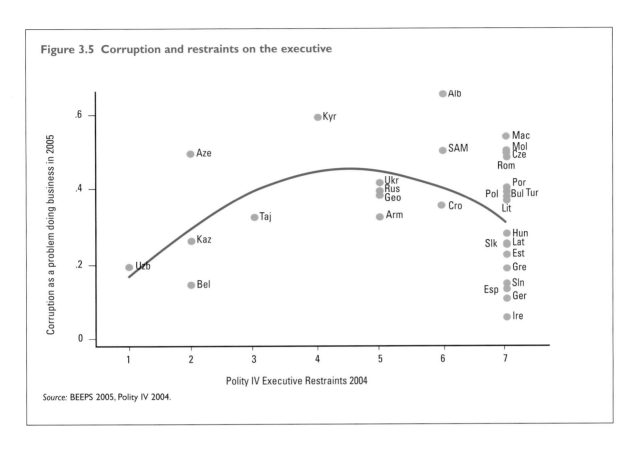

Figure 3.5 Corruption and restraints on the executive

Source: BEEPS 2005, Polity IV 2004.

Among firms that said bribes were sometimes paid, the countries where firms were most likely to say that the amounts were known in advance are almost entirely those identified in the Polity dataset as having deficiencies in restraints on the executive. Only one[19] of the twelve countries with the most predictability in unofficial payments are in the large group with the Polity score equal to 7. Uzbekistan and Belarus are both among the top ten out of 34 countries.

Does all of this imply that reducing the concentration of power by adopting policies that allow greater public dissent, provide the transparency needed to foster political competition, and support economic competition necessarily leads to an increase in the perception of corruption as a problem for business? This could be the case for a few countries, but for most—that is, those that lie on the flat or downward sloping portion of the inverted-U—greater political openness and economic competition can be expected, other things being equal, to reduce corruption. Indeed, most countries that improved on the Freedom

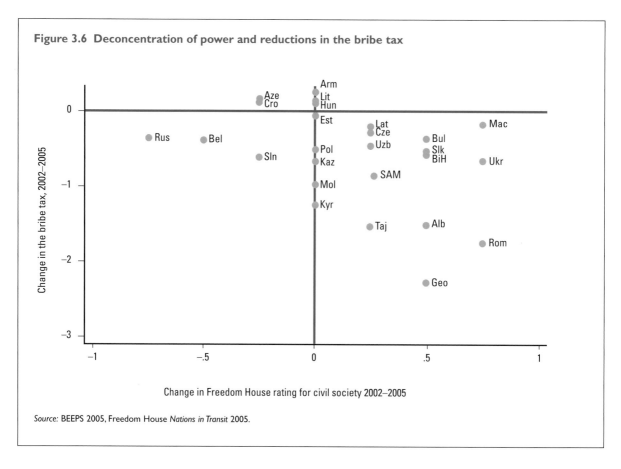

Figure 3.6 Deconcentration of power and reductions in the bribe tax

Source: BEEPS 2005, Freedom House *Nations in Transit* 2005.

House measure of civil society between 2002 and 2005 also saw reductions in the bribe tax (Figure 3.6).[20] Several, including the Slovak Republic and Romania, have emphasized strengthening the hand of civil society and the general public in their anticorruption campaigns. Only three countries—Russia, Belarus, and Slovenia—had both a worsening in the assessment of civil society and a decline in the bribe tax. As explained in Box 3.1 and illustrated for Russia, a decline in the bribe tax does not imply a decline in the absolute level of bribes but rather in the *share* of total revenues paid in bribes. Indeed, in Russia the frequency of bribery stayed at a high level and firms' perception of corruption as a problem for business rose from 2002 and 2005.

As noted at the outset of this section, survey-based measures of corruption in autocratic regimes may be subject to underreporting by firms. Our purpose in this section was not to deny this fact, but to explore alternative explanations for the observed patterns. It is worth noting in this regard that the inverted-U shape described in this section exists even when focusing exclusively on expert opinion measures. Using the Freedom House measure of corruption instead of the BEEPS measures, the pattern becomes steeper and reaches its apex later, but it remains one of an inverted U.[21]

Summary

This chapter looked at a number of factors that could potentially influence the extent of corruption in any given setting. The analysis underscores the importance of firm characteristics: New, private, domestically owned firms are likely to pay the most in bribes (as a share of revenues) and pay bribes the most frequently. Foreign-owned firms pay fewer bribes, as do larger or older firms, state-owned firms, and firms in smaller towns or rural areas. Although patterns vary somewhat by country, these overall results do not bode well for the growth of small and medium enterprises or for private-sector development more generally.

The analysis also underscores the importance of good economic policies and strong institutions in controlling corruption. Committed leaders can make a difference by adopting strong reforms and ensuring their implementation. While richer countries are on average less corrupt than poorer ones, it is not evident that rapid economic growth reduces corruption in the short run. Indeed, there is evidence from the BEEPS panel data that rapid economic growth may exacerbate state capture behavior, perhaps not surprising given the presence of political corruption even in more advanced market economies.

Finally, there is strong evidence from the BEEPS data that the relationship between corruption and political openness follows an inverted U. Firms in the most controlled political and economic settings may perceive less corruption in business relations with the state than countries in the early stages of political and economic liberalization, but corruption is again likely to decline as these systems in transition develop enhanced economic and political competition, more effective institutions of accountability, and stronger constraints on elite power.

Box 3.1 Trends in corruption in Russia

Most observers believe that corruption in Russia has worsened in recent years, although the exact magnitude of recent changes and the severity of the current situation are subjects of continued debate. The Executive Opinion Survey carried out annually by the World Economic Forum (2005) confirms a worsening in experts' perceptions of the governance environment in Russia from 2004 to 2005. Most notable is a decline in perceptions of judicial independence and protection of property rights and an increase in the burden of organized crime on business. Surveys of small businesses undertaken by the Center for Economic and Financial Research (CEFIR, 2005), a Russian think tank, indicate that corruption fell from 2001 to 2002 but then worsened again by 2004. Russian firms that participated in the BEEPS also showed a similar pattern—a dip in assessments of corruption as a problem for business from 1999 to 2002 followed by an increase through 2005. (Reported bribe frequency rose to 2002 and then stayed level.) However, the BEEPS firms—500 in 2002 and nearly 600 in 2005—also reported a decrease in the bribe tax from 1.4 percent of revenues in 2002 to 1.1 percent in 2005. The most negative picture of corruption in Russia was painted last year by another Russian think tank, Information Science for Democracy (INDEM, 2005), which reported that bribes had increased tenfold in the four years from 2001 to 2005.

These various results point in a similar direction—that corruption in Russia may have improved somewhat in the early 2000s but has grown as a problem in recent years. The decline in the bribe tax as measured by the BEEPS is not inconsistent with growth in corruption overall. The bribe tax measures the share of annual revenues paid in bribes, while the INDEM study reports on the aggregate dollar amount of bribes paid per firm per year. Given the rapid growth in the Russian economy in recent years, the declining bribe tax would still translate into a larger volume of bribery, and appreciation of the currency would increase the dollar-equivalent value even further. While the two sources may agree on the direction of change, however, the magnitude of the BEEPS and INDEM results do differ markedly. The BEEPS results imply an approximate increase in the volume of bribery of 50 percent from 2002 to 2005, while the INDEM study reports a staggering growth of nearly 900 percent from 2001–2005.

These worsening trends occurred despite a number of reforms undertaken by the Russian government to streamline public administration. For example, to ease the entry of new firms the government sponsored new legislation in February 2002 that cut the number of activities that required licensing and lowered the cost of obtaining licenses. Similarly, to improve the system of tax administration, the government lowered corporate tax rates and widened tax bases in 2001. Tax revenues increased and compliance clearly improved as a result (Ivanova, Keen, and Klemm, 2005). Yet the BEEPS results indicate that neither the easing of licensing rules nor reductions in tax rates have led to reductions in the frequency of bribery in these areas. Indeed, unofficial payments for business licenses are among the highest in Russia of any transition country, and Doing Business ranks Russia 143 worst out of 155 countries in "dealing with licenses."

One explanation for the seeming failure of policy reforms to reduce corruption may be inconsistent or ineffective implementation of these reforms in practice. As Russia spans two continents and eleven time zones, it is not surprising that both the impacts of specific reforms and trends in corruption appear to vary significantly among regions. The CEFIR report (2005) claims that many business licenses "do not seem to be legitimate" even if they may have gotten cheaper. A second explanation focuses on deterioration in external oversight. Expanding restrictions on the media and some nongovernmental organizations in recent years may have reduced the ability of these groups to disseminate information about government activities and thereby help to hold public officials accountable. A vibrant and diversified civil society with ready access to information is an essential building block for accountability in government.

The results for Russia underscore the fact that policy reforms may be necessary but are not always sufficient to reduce corruption in and of themselves. Fundamental institutional strengthening to ensure policy implementation, build checks and balances, and promote accountability in government is also essential.

See also: World Bank (2005a, 2006c) and www.doingbusiness.org.

Notes

1. In addition to growth, institutions, and politics, we also examined managerial attitudes about corruption. All of the analysis reported here also includes controls for managerial "optimism" in exactly the same manner as in ACT2. This variable was added to the regression analysis in an attempt to remove (or "control for") the impact of systematic biases of individual managers on their survey responses. As noted in the Annex, the constructed variable measured the difference between a manager's view of the extent of macroeconomic stability in a country and the actual extent of macroeconomic stability in that country (as measured by objective economic data). Managers who reported that the economy was more stable than the data showed were said to be optimistic, while those who saw the economy as less stable than the data showed were pessimistic. The hypothesis was that a person's optimism or pessimism may affect all of his/her answers in the survey, and adjusting the BEEPS variables on corruption by this optimism/pessimism variable could lead to a more accurate comparison of reality across firms. Indeed, the optimism/pessimism variable was highly significant in 2002 and is again highly significant in virtually all regressions in 2005. More optimistic managers report better results—that is, lower corruption—on every relevant variable, which shows that there is likely to be some subjective bias in individual's answers. Moreover, some countries tend to have a large number of optimistic managers while others tend toward the pessimistic, no doubt a reflection in part of the prevailing national mood. However, it is worth stressing that the results discussed in this chapter for other variables—including the effects of firm characteristics and the positive impact of better policies and institutions on the level of corruption—all reflect conclusions after correcting for this optimism/pessimism variable.

2. ACT2 (World Bank 2004), Chapter 3.

3. See the Methodological Annex for regression results.

4. As the figure focuses on the extremes, the numbers of observations per country per year can be small. The figure therefore shows the simple averages across all firms (rather than across countries) in a given year for transition and nontransition countries, respectively.

5. See, for example, Treisman (2000) and Mauro (1995).

6. A large body of recent literature attempts to unravel the effects of corruption on either the level or the rate of economic growth. Some recent research that attempts to use instrumental variables to address the simultaneity problems finds that corruption leads to lower GDP per

capita. See, for example, Mauro (1995), Hall and Jones (1999), Kaufmann, Kraay, and Zoido- Lobatón (1999), and Kaufmann and Kraay (2002).

7. Ades and Di Tella (1999).

8. See description in ACT2 (World Bank 2004). As the 2005 CPIA scores came after and were influenced by the 2005 BEEPS data, we used the 2004 CPIA scores in this analysis. The CPIA indicator on "Transparency, Accountability, and Corruption in the Public Sector" was not used as the results would be tautological.

9. Freedom House *Nations in Transit* (http://www.freedomhouse.org) was chosen for this exercise since the assessments are publicly available and are accompanied by narratives justifying the ratings. While about 30 percent of the variation in the Freedom House corruption measure can be explained by bribe frequency and bribe tax, less than 10 percent can be explained by the BEEPS assessments of corruption as a problem doing business.

10. European Bank for Reconstruction and Development (2005).

11. A survey of the general public in late 2004 similarly found the perception of corruption levels in Belarus to be lower than in other transition countries. Rose (2005) reports that 67 percent of respondents in Belarus stated that "most public officials are corrupt," compared to 74 percent for the new EU members, and 88 percent for Russia.

12. Hellman, Jones, and Kaufmann (2000), cited in World Bank (2000).

13. Such inverted-U's also appear in nonempirical discussions of the links between political systems and corruption. Alina Mungiu-Pippidi (forthcoming) focuses on the distribution of power in a society and presents a chart showing corruption to have an inverted-U relationship with the distribution of power in political systems. The Romanian political scientist asks what corruption means in repressive systems where the existence and operation of the state is geared entirely toward the benefit of the leader, as in a monarchy or dictatorship. It makes little sense, she argues, to talk about "abuse of position" when it is really just "use of system" according to the rules of that system. In this framework, corruption, as defined by abuse of position, would be low in countries with high concentrations of political power and in countries where diffuse power-sharing arrangements serve to restrain the executive, but higher for countries with mixed systems that lack effective restraints on the state. This is similar to the argument in *Anticorruption in Transition* (World Bank 2000)—that the concentration of power and lack of restraints that characterized the emergence from communism were responsible for taking corruption to new levels and in a new direction.

14. The Freedom House *Nations in Transit* assessment of civil society "assesses the growth of nongovernmental organizations, their organiza-

tional capacity and financial sustainability, and the legal and political environment in which they function. Also considers the development of free trade unions; interest group participation in the policy process; the freedom of educational systems from political influence and propaganda; and the freedom of society from excessive influence from extremist and intolerant nongovernmental institutions and organizations" (Freedom House 2005).

15. Both coefficients on the civil society assessment and its square are significant at the 1 percent level.

16. The coefficients are virtually unchanged when these two countries are dropped, while the significance level falls from the 1 percent level to the 5 percent level.

17. Information on the Polity IV Project can be found at http://www.cidcm .umd.edu/inscr/polity/#data.

18. Interestingly, however, managers of foreign-owned firms in the countries (that is, another type of "foreign" observer) report slightly lower levels of corruption than their domestic counterparts.

19. Hungary was the only country with a Polity assessment of restraints on the executive equal to 7 among the 12 countries with the highest percentage of firms indicating that bribes are sometimes paid and the amounts are known in advance.

20. The pattern evident in Figure 3.6 is similar, but statistically weaker, for bribe frequency.

21. Using quadratics of both the Freedom House civil society measure and the Polity IV measure of executive restraints on the right hand side, the quadratic pattern is statistically significant and in both cases Belarus and Uzbekistan lie on the portion of the curve beyond the apex.

4

Policies and Corruption Outcomes

CHAPTER 2 ESTABLISHED THAT BROAD INDICATORS OF CORRUPTION, as reported by the business community, have declined in many transition countries in the 3-year period from 2002 to 2005, continuing the trend of the three earlier years. Chapter 3 analyzed the relationships of these corruption trends to several broad features of the firms surveyed and the institutional and political environment. This chapter looks more closely at specific types of corruption and how they are influenced by public policies and institutions. To be successful in an anticorruption drive, leaders need to understand where corruption occurs and what government actions might influence it. Recent reforms in policies and institutions in some transition countries provide guidance on what steps might help.

Figure 4.1 summarizes the trends in corruption in specific areas from 2002 and 2005 for transition countries and compares the results with nontransition countries.[1] Congruent with the findings in Chapter 2, firms in transition countries reported significant reductions in corruption in the regulatory environment, access to utilities, and tax and customs administration. However, for the region as a whole corruption did not improve for the courts or public procurement. The extent of state capture—that is, payments to influence the design (as opposed to the implementation) of laws and government regulations—appears mostly unchanged.[2] In every area, however, the average frequency of bribery in transition countries remains significantly higher than the average for nontransition countries.[3]

Understanding the reasons for progress requires some examination of the policy environment. While there are several choices of indicators on corruption, including surveys such as BEEPS and expert opinions such as those produced by Freedom House, there are relatively fewer sources of indicators on the policy environment. In this section, we draw on a dataset produced by the World Bank called "Doing Business" to examine how official laws, rules, and procedures affect the frequency of bribery as reported by firms in specific sectors. Box 4.1 clarifies why Doing Business and BEEPS are complementary tools. The analysis covers all of the sectors surveyed by the BEEPS for which there is a direct analogue on the policy side from Doing Business. We also draw on indicators of the institutional and policy environment provided by the World Bank's CPIA and indicators of specific anticorruption measures collected by other researchers to get a sense of the degree to which cross-cutting reforms influence the levels of corruption. The analysis is supplemented by the World Bank's experience in helping countries on the ground with policy reforms and institutional strengthening in the various areas discussed.

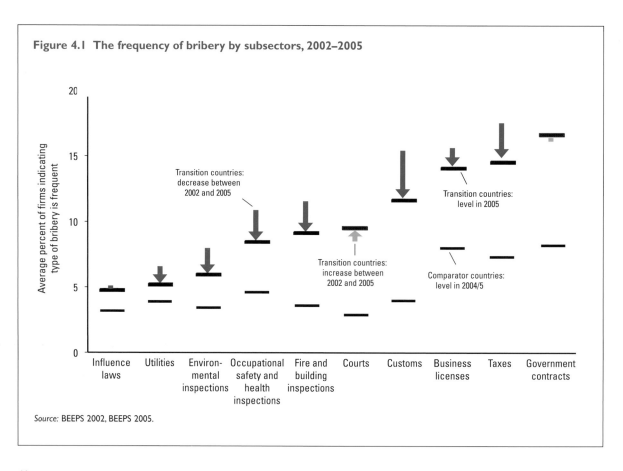

Figure 4.1 The frequency of bribery by subsectors, 2002–2005

Source: BEEPS 2002, BEEPS 2005.

In reviewing the apparent relationships between policies and corruption outcomes, an important caveat should be stated up front. Much of the analysis relies on cross-country patterns of contemporaneous indicators of both policies and corruption. While the approach is a static one, a dynamic interpretation is projected based on the cross-sectional patterns. In terms of long-run relationships, this is a reasonable approach. Complications may arise, however, when the relationship between policies and outcomes is subject to long lags, or is influenced by reverse causality or by the existence of additional factors that influence both policies and corruption outcomes.[4]

Box 4.1 The relationship between the BEEPS and the Doing Business indicators

The BEEPS and the World Bank Group's "Doing Business" are complementary efforts to examine the environments in which firms do business. They use different methodologies and answer related, but different, questions.

Most of the Doing Business indicators are generated by asking lawyers, accountants, and other professionals in each country about the details of the laws, rules, and procedures that govern various aspects of doing business. In order to ensure cross-country comparability, the Doing Business methodology presents hypothetical cases or situations that are the same for each country, and the cases are assumed to be taking place in the largest city. Doing Business can be thought of as a compilation of indicators about various government policies, rules, and procedures.

The BEEPS, in contrast, asks 200–600 firms throughout each country questions about their business environment and their interactions with the state. The samples are chosen in a uniform way in each country, with sector composition divided according to contribution to GDP. The BEEPS can be thought of as a compilation of indicators about what firms are saying about the ways that government policies, rules, and procedures are implemented in practice.

Often, Doing Business and BEEPS suggest the same trends. Doing Business in 2006 highlighted several countries in Europe and Central Asia as leading reformers, and the BEEPS 2005 results also suggest improvement over the past three years in some of the same countries. In countries where the results do not seem congruent, there are many possible explanations. Firms may have found ways to work around problematic regulations so that they are less burdensome; conversely, the formal rules and procedures may appear benign, while nontransparent implementation may cause firms considerable difficulty. In addition, improvements captured in the Doing Business indicators may take time to be recognized by the business community. For example, reductions in minimum capital requirements to start a company will not help the firms that are already in existence.

For further information see World Bank 2006c: www.doingbusiness.org.

Taxation

An important area where it appears that solid progress is being made in the fight against corruption is tax administration. Although still a concern, far fewer firms in transition countries report that bribes are frequent in the tax system (Figure 4.2). Among individual countries the most striking improvements from 2002 to 2005 were in Georgia, where the percentage of firms reporting that bribery of tax officials was frequent fell from 44 percent to 11 percent in these three years. Marked improvements from relatively high levels of corruption are evident Bosnia and Herzegovina, Moldova, Tajikistan, and Ukraine; and more modest improvements are evident from lower starting points in FYR Macedonia, Romania, and the Slovak Republic. Bribery appears to have worsened from already high levels in the Kyrgyz Republic, from more moderate

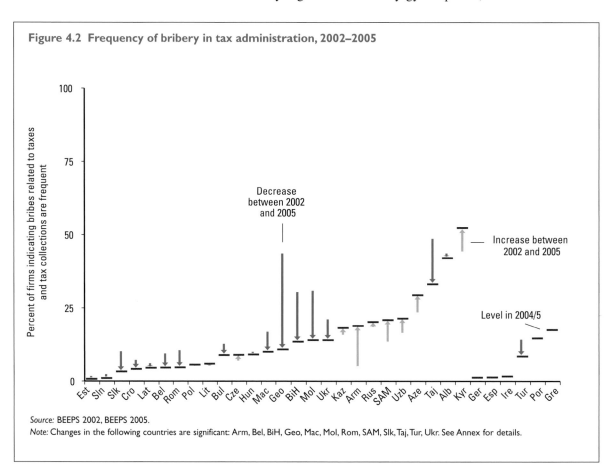

Figure 4.2 Frequency of bribery in tax administration, 2002–2005

Source: BEEPS 2002, BEEPS 2005.
Note: Changes in the following countries are significant: Arm, Bel, BiH, Geo, Mac, Mol, Rom, SAM, Slk, Taj, Tur, Ukr. See Annex for details.

levels in Serbia and Montenegro, and from previously low levels in Armenia. Of the comparator countries, corruption in the tax system appears relatively higher in Greece and Portugal, moderate in Turkey, and very low in Germany, Ireland, and Spain.

While the details of policies and institutional design matter, a simple association exists between corruption levels on the one hand and the degree to which the tax system is a burden on the other (Figure 4.3). Countries where firms make paying taxes simpler and easier tend to have lower levels of corruption related to taxes.[5]

The positive results in many transition countries are correlated with aggressive reforms over the past few years to simplify tax policy and tax administration. On the tax policy side, transition countries have been worldwide leaders in adopting simplified low- or flat-rate income taxes with broad bases and few exemptions. The flat tax took effect first in

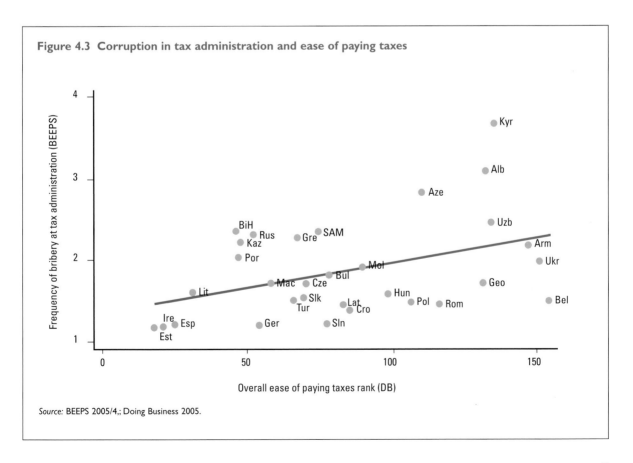

Figure 4.3 Corruption in tax administration and ease of paying taxes

Source: BEEPS 2005/4,; Doing Business 2005.

Estonia in 1994, followed by Lithuania (1994), Latvia (1995), Russia (2001), the Slovak Republic (2004), Ukraine (2004), Georgia (2005), and Romania (2005). The Slovak Republic's experience with tax reform is described in Box 4.2. Even where income tax rates are not entirely flat, there tend to be fewer rate brackets with relatively low top rates (typically in the teens or low 20s). Armenia's corporate and top personal income tax rates, for example, are both 20 percent, and Poland's corporate and small business tax rates are both 19 percent. There have also been reforms in indirect taxes. Value-added taxes (typically at a uniform rate) have replaced the turnover taxes inherited from socialist times and generally account for a large and growing share of revenues. While the VAT is a formidable revenue raiser (particularly at rates in the high teens that are typical in the region), VAT refunds have proven to be difficult to implement smoothly in most settings and are one source of significant corruption. Arguably the most pressing current tax policy issue relates to labor taxes (including social contributions), which continue to be very high in most transition settings. These rates create tax "wedges"—the difference between the cost of labor to the employer and the take-home pay of the employee—of up to 50 percent, contributing to the relatively low rates of formal employment in many transition countries.[6]

Reforms in tax policy and improvements in tax administration can be mutually reinforcing, and many of the countries that have undertaken major tax policy reforms are benefiting from improved administration and lower corruption. However, one does not necessarily lead to the other, and thus it is important for governments to focus on both areas simultaneously. Many transition countries are undertaking far-reaching reforms to improve their tax administration services and promote greater transparency and efficiency. Most have moved to a functional organization to consolidate the same processes (assessment, collection, appeals, and so forth) for different taxes under one group. In some cases, such as Bulgaria, the collection of taxes and social contributions have recently been merged to increase compliance and reduce superfluous audits (which themselves create opportunities for corruption). Countries have established "Large Taxpayer Units," which have proven very effective in mobilizing resources from large companies and other major taxpayers in their countries. They have introduced unique taxpayer numbers, taxpayer self-assessment procedures, and information technology (IT) systems for electronic filing and data collection, all of which help to reduce discretion and direct contact between taxpayers and tax officials while enhancing efficiency and transparency

Box 4.2 Tax reform in the Slovak Republic

One of the key reforms undertaken in the Slovak Republic in recent years is the 2004 reform of the tax and benefits system. The reform introduced a relatively low flat-rate tax and reformed the system of social benefits. Although the reform was praised by many for its positive impact on competitiveness, concerns were voiced about its potential negative effect on poverty and income distribution. A detailed evaluation of the reforms found, however, that the move to a flat-rate tax made the tax system more rather than less progressive. Furthermore, overall tax collections were not significantly affected, and the BEEPS data show that firms' perceptions of the tax system have improved markedly, that tax evasion is falling, and that bribes related to taxes are paid less frequently.

Tax rates as a problem doing business

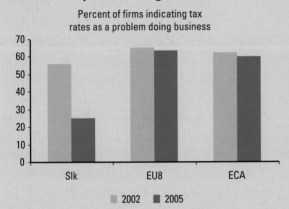

Tax administration as a problem doing business

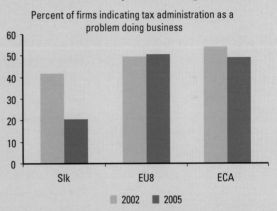

Annual sales reported for tax purposes

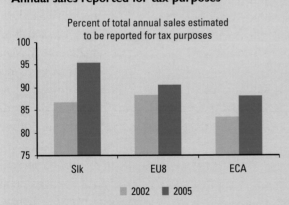

Unofficial payments for tax collection

The tax reforms did not come in isolation. The Slovak Republic has also adopted many other sector-specific and cross-cutting reforms. As with many other countries that have shown improvement, both in specific sectors and across the board, the Slovak Republic led reforms through the implementation of a freedom-of-information law, effectively making civil society and the general public allies in the fight against corruption.

Sources: BEEPS 2002, 2005; World Bank 2005c.

throughout the tax system. Audits and enforcement have also been stepped up or made more efficient, including in some cases (most notably Georgia and Ukraine) large-scale replacement of managers and staff in the tax service and increases in the salaries for tax officials. Tax administration remains weakest in some of the poorer countries in the region, such as the Kyrgyz Republic and Tajikistan, where resources are tight and policy and institutional reforms are not as advanced.

Customs

As with tax, the BEEPS results also point to significant reductions from 2002 to 2005 in customs-related bribery for many transition countries (Figure 4.4). Country-specific patterns of changes in customs-related bribery are similar to those in the tax system, with major improvements in Bosnia and Herzegovina, Bulgaria, Georgia, FYR Macedonia, Moldova, Romania, the Slovak Republic, and Tajikistan, and some deterioration in Armenia. Among the comparator countries, Portugal and Turkey appear to have levels of corruption in customs that are comparable to most of the new EU members, while bribery in customs appears to be very low in Germany, Greece, Ireland, and Spain. By far the highest levels of corruption in customs are reported in Albania, where 44 percent of firms report that bribery is frequent.

The marked reduction in customs-related bribery in many transition countries is not particularly surprising given the concerted efforts that are being made to improve customs administrations. Virtually all countries have revised their customs legislation, often in line with EU standards and with EU assistance. Most countries have invested in new information technology to increase efficiency and transparency. Not only does this allow greater information sharing among relevant government agencies and customs sites, but it also allows customs administration to become increasingly paperless, giving both traders and customs officials the ability to handle documents and track progress on-line. Customs administrations in the region are also moving to risk-based assessment and more selective auditing, which reduces discretion in the selection of items for physical inspection. Croatia, for example, has fully rolled out selectivity and risk management techniques and has reduced the number of physical exams extensively, and the results on the corruption front appear very promising. Albania and Moldova have introduced IT and the

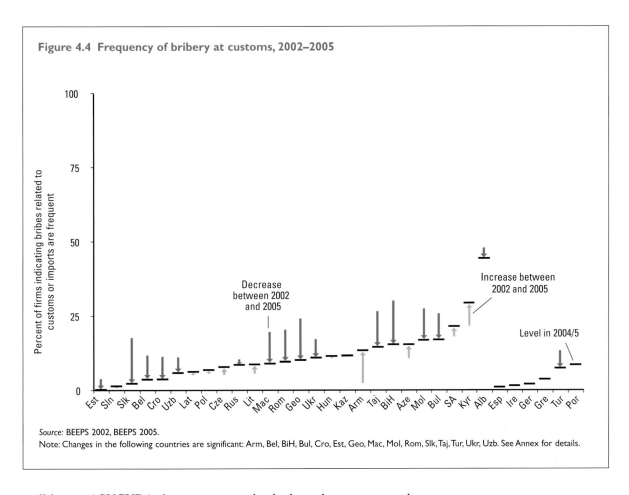

Figure 4.4 Frequency of bribery at customs, 2002–2005

Source: BEEPS 2002, BEEPS 2005.

Note: Changes in the following countries are significant: Arm, Bel, BiH, Bul, Cro, Est, Geo, Mac, Mol, Rom, Slk, Taj, Tur, Ukr, Uzb. See Annex for details.

well-known ASYCUDA clearance system, but both need to move toward greater selectivity and risk assessment. Although firms in Serbia and Montenegro reported no significant change in the frequency of bribery at customs between 2002 and 2005, reforms focusing on transparency, simplified procedures, and monitoring have accelerated in the past year.

Where systemic corruption is widespread, strong sanctions may also be needed to change staffing and expectations. For example, the new Georgian government that took office after the Rose Revolution moved quickly to replace many managers and staff in the customs and tax administrations, and the Slovak Republic has set up a criminal office in the customs service to strengthen the detection and investigation of fraud and corruption. The strong and concerted efforts to address corruption in both countries appear to be paying off. In addition, some countries (such as FYR Macedonia) have introduced internal audit or ethics departments in their customs services to focus more directly on broad strategies for combating corruption.

Given the cross-national nature of customs work, international cooperation can help improve the efficacy of reforms. One example is the project on Trade and Transport Facilitation in southeast Europe (TTFSE), which aims to streamline customs procedures and improve efficiency at border crossings in eight southeast European countries (see Box 4.3). A key element of the program is the system of detailed monitoring of customs clearance times at the pilot borders, and nearly every border crossing shows a trend of dramatic improvement. This finding is also borne out in the BEEPS—the southeast Europe region showed more improvement in levels of bribery at customs than any other region.

As with taxation, reforms in policy and administration can be mutually reinforcing in the area of customs. Not only do low and uniform tariffs reduce uncertainty and room for bargaining over tariff rates with customs officials, but they also induce a higher volume of trade and thus more pressure for efficiency in customs administration. Although the findings of academic research are not unanimous, there is some evidence that more open and liberal trade regimes are correlated with lower levels of corruption.[7] Most transition countries (other than Belarus, Turkmenistan, and Uzbekistan) have reduced tariffs and now have quite liberal trade policy regimes, with low average tariffs and few nontariff barriers.[8] Of course the level of tariffs and nontariff barriers at the border is only part of the story, as "behind the border" administrative regulations and other restrictive domestic policies can also stifle international trade. Reducing the often-large number of required precustoms permits, registrations, and licenses, and clarifying and simplifying technical regulations are critical steps in removing opportunities and incentives for corruption.

Figure 4.5 shows the relationship between the frequency of bribery in customs and the Doing Business indicator for the ease of trading across borders, which is based mostly on the administrative burden for firms in dealing with customs. The relationship between policies, institutions, and the level of bribery is again evident.

Judicial systems

In contrast to tax and customs, the BEEPS results do not point to an overall decline in corruption in the judicial systems in transition

Box 4.3 International cooperation in customs reform—trade and transport facilitation in Southeast Europe

The southeast Europe subregion stands out as the one where bribes to customs officials are most frequent, yet also where bribes have declined the most. As every border crossing involves two countries, international cooperation may be necessary for effective reforms. The project on Trade and Transport Facilitation in Southeast Europe (TTFSE), a collaborative effort between eight national governments, the World Bank, the United States, and the European Union, seeks to reduce nontariff costs of transport, reduce corruption at borders, combine modernization of customs administration with institutional reform, and bring transparency to border crossing procedures.

Surveys of truck drivers in 2001 and 2002 asked about typical bribe payments when crossing borders. In Albania, 96 percent of trucks said they paid bribes to customs officials, while in Bulgaria 24 percent said likewise—the other countries fell in between. The bribe amounts ranged from a high of 342 Euros reported by Albanian drivers to a low of 23 reported by Romanian drivers. Payments were made most frequently in Moldova, where 82 percent of border crossings involved a bribe. Thus the challenge faced by the project was formidable.

There has been considerable success to date. The project places a premium on monitoring, tracking clearance times for each of the border crossings. For nearly every crossing the average trend has been favorable, and clearance times have declined sharply at many of the border crossings. Trends for two of them are depicted below.

Bosnia and Herzegovina, Federation, Izacic. Entry times

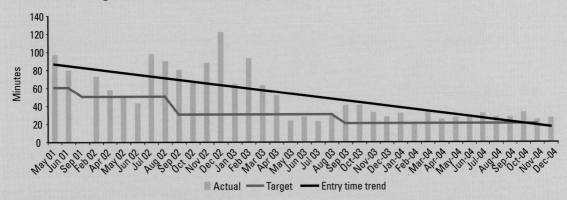

Romania, Constanta. Clearance times

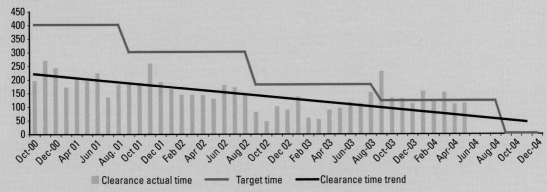

Source: The Website of TTFSE (http://www.seerecon.org/ttfse/), and PlanConsult (2003).

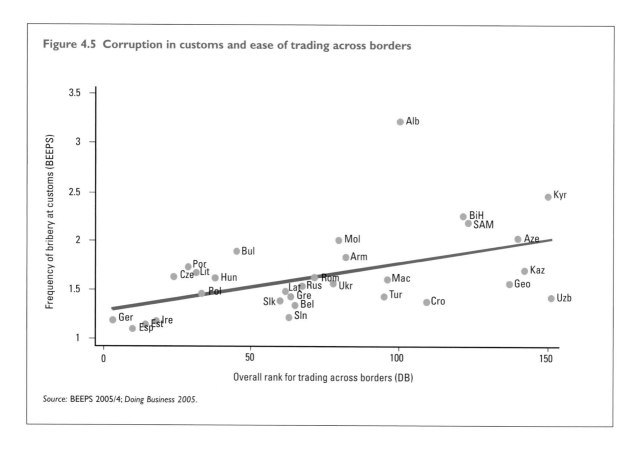

Figure 4.5 Corruption in customs and ease of trading across borders

Source: BEEPS 2005/4; Doing Business 2005.

countries, although there is progress in some countries. Figure 4.6 shows the percent of firms reporting in 2002 and 2005 that bribery in courts is frequent. The firms in the survey report less frequent bribery in the courts than three years ago in a few countries, including Georgia, Romania, and the Slovak Republic, but more frequent bribes in others, most notably Albania and Serbia and Montenegro (and, from a low base, Armenia). One does not see the improvements in Bulgaria, Moldova, FYR Macedonia, or Ukraine that were evident in tax and customs.

What would it take to establish true accountability in the judiciary? A myriad of individual steps are needed, including (i) ensuring merit-based systems for judicial appointment, promotion, and disciplinary proceedings, as well as adequate judicial salaries and training; (ii) promoting transparency in all judicial proceedings through open access to court hearings by the public the media and through publication of judicial decisions; and (iii) prosecution of some high-profile corruption cases, whether in the judiciary or in government more broadly. Only through

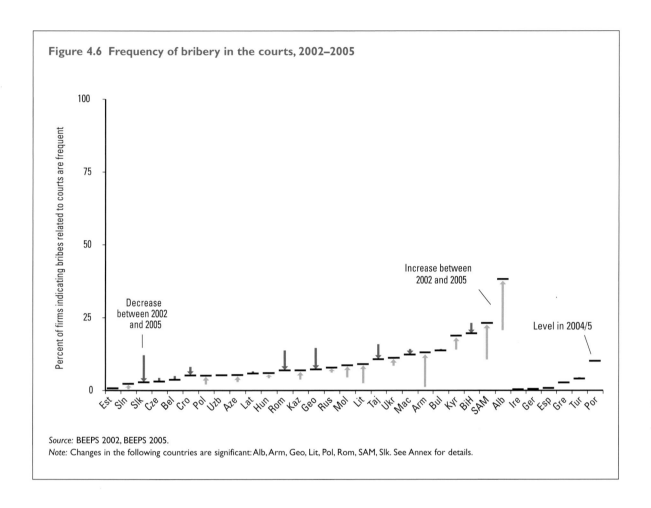

Figure 4.6 Frequency of bribery in the courts, 2002–2005

Source: BEEPS 2002, BEEPS 2005.
Note: Changes in the following countries are significant: Alb, Arm, Geo, Lit, Pol, Rom, SAM, Slk. See Annex for details.

the "carrot" of professional stature and remuneration and the "stick" of potential punishment for wrongdoing—together with the incentives and self-enforcement mechanisms that arise from transparency—can corruption be successfully tackled.

Judiciaries and governments are aware of the dismal stigma of corruption, and significant steps are being taken to address it in many countries.[9] In Romania and Russia, for example, judicial salaries have been raised substantially to a level that compares reasonably to average private-sector salaries. This move has raised the status of the profession, its "value" to incumbents, and its attractiveness to potential candidates. The process of judicial selection is also being tightened, and training opportunities for judges are being expanded. Georgia, for example, was one of the first countries to introduce examinations for judges, and other transition countries have followed suit. Georgia and Armenia have also adopted nationwide merit-based exams for entrance to law schools in an effort to reduce corruption at this entry point into the profession. While these examination processes are themselves not without difficulties, they are a step in the right direction compared to selection processes of old. As a complement to merit-based selection of judges, the Slovak Republic has put major efforts into strengthening government's capacity to prosecute cases of judicial corruption, including setting up a special court and prosecution office to deal with cases of corruption and organized crime.

Transition countries are also taking important steps to teach citizens[10] about their rights and to increase the transparency of the legal system. In Armenia, a television show called "My Rights," in which a government official plays the role of a judge hearing cases, has become popular and is now in its second year of production. In Russia, the government set up a network of "Legal Information Centers" in public libraries and other locations in the late 1990s, where the public can access information on laws and the justice system. In Croatia (and many other transition countries), the courts are adopting an automated case-management system that will not only improve efficiency but also produce better statistical data to monitor performance. Countries' judiciaries and ministries of justice throughout the region are establishing wide-area networks to connect courts and websites to publicize laws, judicial calendars, and decisions in individual cases.

Finally, corruption in the judiciary can be reduced through deregulation and other legal reforms that reduce the number of encounters that firms and private citizens must have with judges and other court personnel. Figure 4.7 points to the significant correlation between the number of procedures required to enforce a contract and the extent of bribery in the judiciary. Overall, the findings with respect to the judiciary support those of earlier research underscoring that judicial reform deserves focused attention.[11]

Government procurement

As in the courts, government procurement is another area where levels of bribery are relatively high and do not appear to be improving in many countries (Figure 4.8). While the average "kickback tax"—the percent-

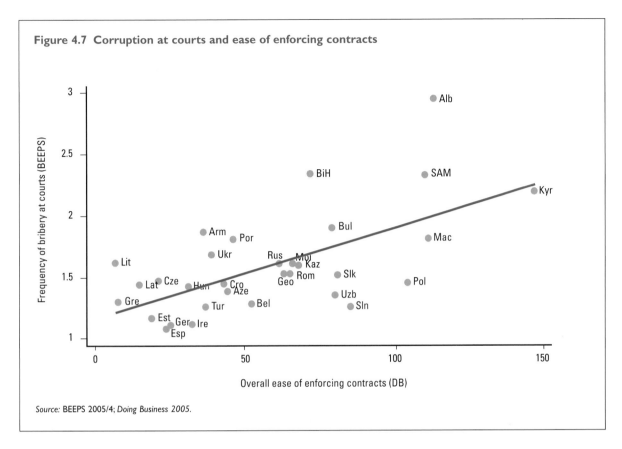

Figure 4.7 Corruption at courts and ease of enforcing contracts

Source: BEEPS 2005/4; *Doing Business 2005.*

age of contract value that firms say they must pay to secure government contracts—has declined for the region as a whole, the frequency with which firms say they bribe for government contracts has not. In some countries with low or improving levels of corruption in other areas— most notably Estonia and Georgia and also Bosnia and Herzegovina, Romania, Tajikistan, and Ukraine—firms also report declining frequency of bribery in public procurement between 2002 and 2005. However, firms in some of the richer and otherwise less corrupt countries in the sample— including the Czech Republic and Lithuania—report growing levels of bribery in government procurement and among the highest levels of such bribery in the region. Firms in the wealthier comparator countries (most notably Germany) also report significant levels of corruption in public procurement, indicating that this is a particularly difficult problem for governments to address.[12] For larger procurements, the potential bribes may well be large enough to have political implications, and thus corruption in public procurement may shade into state capture.

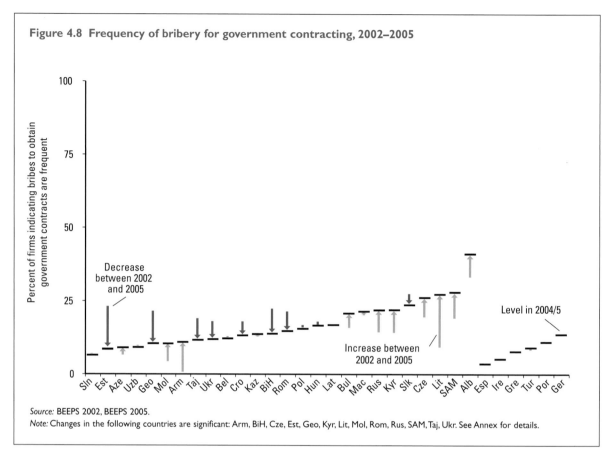

Figure 4.8 Frequency of bribery for government contracting, 2002–2005

Source: BEEPS 2002, BEEPS 2005.
Note: Changes in the following countries are significant: Arm, BiH, Cze, Est, Geo, Kyr, Lit, Mol, Rom, Rus, SAM, Taj, Ukr. See Annex for details.

Many governments are trying to improve the efficiency and transparency of their public procurement processes. Many have passed new procurement laws and established state procurement agencies with clearer and more transparent operating rules. Centralizing procurement has been helpful in some settings, but a decentralized model can also work (and may even be preferable) if backed by a solid legislative framework and a comprehensive capacity-building program. Following the lead of OECD and more advanced developing countries (such as Mexico and Chile), a number of transition countries (such as Armenia) are moving to e-procurement, using public websites to disseminate tenders, accept bids, and announce results.

While increasing efficiency and transparency can no doubt make a difference, tackling the full range of corruption in public procurement is likely to entail deeper political reforms in many instances. Moreover, this area of reform is prone to backsliding, because it depends on consistent application of transparent and standardized rules for competitive procurement. Countries may adopt world-class procurement laws but apply them in an inconsistent manner, or may adopt subsequent laws exempting some procurement from the standards and thereby weakening their effectiveness.

As a whole, progress in reducing corruption related to government procurement has been disappointing.[13] While there were large improvements in a few countries, the number of countries where corruption got worse in this area is also large. The decline in the magnitude of the kickback tax reflects large improvements in a small number of countries, and the frequency with which firms say they bribe for government contracts remains worrisome. As the region continues to develop and larger investment projects become more feasible, the potential rents in government procurement will keep pace. Even in the most advanced countries with sophisticated procurement systems, corruption scandals often surround procurement transactions. Indeed, some of the European comparators have higher levels of unofficial payments related to procurement than several of the transition countries. Improving procurement systems—focusing on transparency, competition, and standardization—must be a key priority for governance reforms in the coming years.

Regulatory environment

Firms in Europe and Central Asia have been calling for reductions in red tape and bureaucracy for years, and many countries have begun to address these pleas. *Doing Business in 2006* (World Bank 2006c) highlighted the region as the leader in adopting reforms that make it easier for firms to do business. The average "time tax," a rudimentary indicator from the BEEPS of the amount of time senior managers spend dealing with public officials, has declined significantly across the region.[14] So, too, has the propensity to encounter bribery when dealing with business licensing or inspections, as is clear from Figure 4.9. Across countries, however, business licensing continues to be one of the areas most beset by unofficial payments. One example is Russia (see Box 3.1), where laws were adopted in 2002 to reduce the number of activities requiring licenses and to cut the cost of obtaining such licenses. However, various recent surveys conclude that these legislative changes, while having some positive impact in the first year, have not resulted in lasting

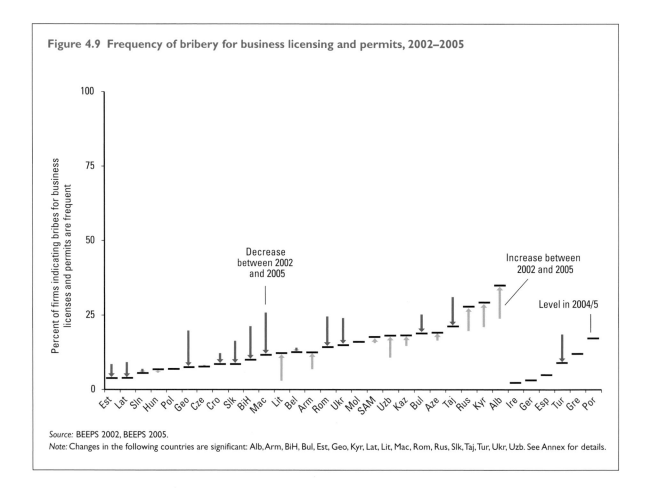

Figure 4.9 Frequency of bribery for business licensing and permits, 2002–2005

Source: BEEPS 2002, BEEPS 2005.
Note: Changes in the following countries are significant: Alb, Arm, BiH, Bul, Est, Geo, Kyr, Lat, Lit, Mac, Rom, Rus, Slk, Taj, Tur, Ukr, Uzb. See Annex for details.

reductions in the burdens of licensing and associated bribery on businesses.

Doing Business provides support for the importance of including reforms in business licensing in an anticorruption strategy. Unofficial payments are lower in countries that make it easier for firms to deal with licenses (Figure 4.10). Similarly, Figure 4.11 shows that, on average, countries with less frequent inspections (using occupational health and safety inspections as an example) have fewer unofficial payments. Of course, most types of inspections serve a public purpose, so the goal should not be merely to reduce numbers but to rationalize the system of inspections so that they achieve their purpose without unduly burdening firms and opening greater opportunities for corruption. Moreover, reducing the number of regulations without simultaneously establishing

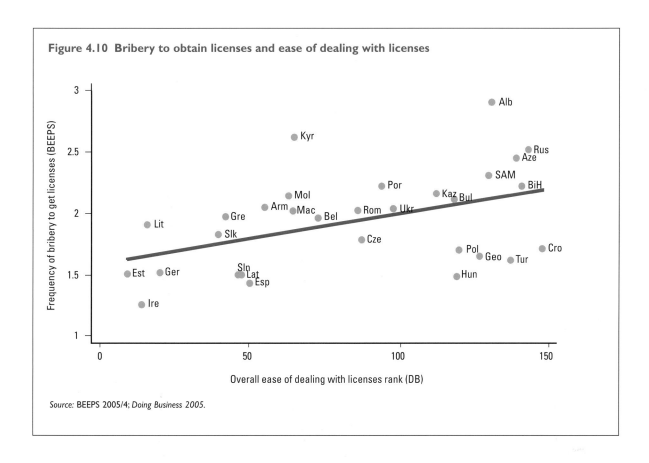

Figure 4.10 **Bribery to obtain licenses and ease of dealing with licenses**

Source: BEEPS 2005/4; *Doing Business 2005.*

a mechanism to vet upcoming draft regulations may lead to only short-lived successes. In the Kyrgyz Republic, for example, many regulations were eliminated in the past five years, only to be reintroduced later. While removing regulations might be relatively easy, reforming the process through which regulations are drafted, evaluated, and publicly discussed is a much deeper—and more challenging—institutional reform.

Cross-cutting reforms

Apart from the specific areas of reforms described above, countries can adopt a wide variety of cross-cutting policy and institutional reforms to strengthen public-sector performance. Improving bureaucratic efficiency through public administration reforms has been a staple of such efforts. Although targeted at improving performance generally rather than

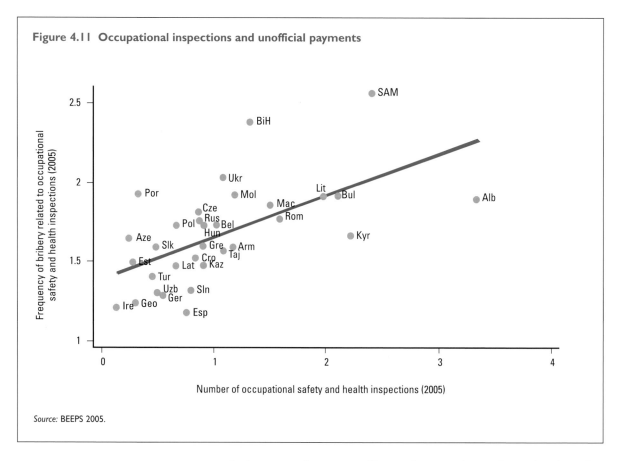

Figure 4.11 Occupational inspections and unofficial payments

Source: BEEPS 2005.

reducing corruption per se, efforts to improve the meritocratic orientation of the civil service are increasing viewed as important steps in the long-run process of reducing corruption.[15] Similarly, fiscal transparency is correlated with lower levels of corruption.[16] Many reformers have also sought to reduce corruption through broader efforts to promote transparency and mechanisms for citizen redress. These include, among other measures, conflict of interest laws and asset declaration rules for public officials, freedom of information laws, and the establishment of supreme audit institutions, ombudsman offices, and anticorruption commissions. Some countries have instituted hotlines and other confidential avenues for citizen complaints. Often these laws are elements of national anticorruption strategies.

The paucity of systematic information on anticorruption institutions has, until recently, made it hard to analyze (except anecdotally) the effectiveness of many cross-cutting anticorruption reforms.[17] Two recent studies have begun to change that by systematically collecting information on anticorruption measures in transition countries. Steves and Rousso (2003), focusing on the period from 1999 to 2002, collected information on the adoption of laws in transition countries addressing freedom of information, civil service, political party finance, anti-money laundering, and so forth, as well as details on anticorruption strategies and status with regard to international conventions. They found that the adoption of laws was associated with declines in many forms of corruption, although adoption of an anticorruption strategy (without targeted legislative components) was not significantly associated with changes in corruption between 1999 and 2002. A more recent update (Rousso and Steves 2005) examined changes between 2002 and 2005 and found no links between the anticorruption policies that were adopted between 1999 and 2002 and the subsequent changes in corruption.[18]

A second data collection effort provides a needed time series. Dorhoi (2005) collected information on many anticorruption institutions in nine policy areas for 15 transition countries[19] for three specific points in time: 1999, 2002, and 2003. Using a detailed scoring system, qualitative assessments of the virtues of the laws resulted in indexes of quality with a ten representing the best possible score.[20] Figure 4.12 shows the average score across all 15 countries for both 1995 and 2003. Clearly, this was a period of much activity in many countries, with the exception of the area of immunities.

Such measures cannot be very effective without strong leadership and other mutually-supporting reforms.[21] Albania, for example, has instituted many cross-cutting anticorruption reforms, and has among the highest scores for the indexes created by Rousso and Steves and by Dorhoi. The BEEPS results did not point to progress on anticorruption through the spring of 2005, when the survey was conducted, although the new government has committed to address the problem with renewed intensity. In contrast, Romania has undertaken many of these reforms under strong pressure from the EU, apparently with significant success (see Box 4.4).[22]

The success of anticorruption strategies also varies, a key theme of the Rousso and Steves (2005) analysis. Armenia developed an Anticorruption Strategy and Action Plan in 2003 and created a high-level Anticorruption Council chaired by the Prime Minister in 2004, but the 2005 BEEPS results were significantly worse along many dimensions of corruption than the 2002 results. In contrast, Georgia also adopted a

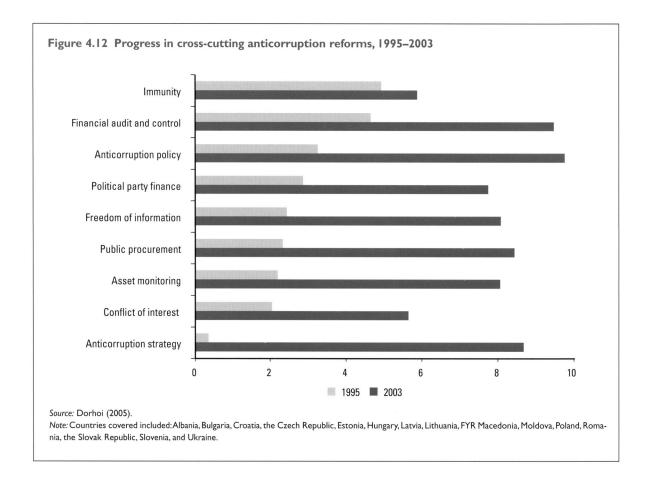

Figure 4.12 Progress in cross-cutting anticorruption reforms, 1995–2003

Source: Dorhoi (2005).

Note: Countries covered included: Albania, Bulgaria, Croatia, the Czech Republic, Estonia, Hungary, Latvia, Lithuania, FYR Macedonia, Moldova, Poland, Romania, the Slovak Republic, Slovenia, and Ukraine.

National Anticorruption Strategy and Action Plan, but it was accompanied by (or in some cases followed by) a large array of policy and institutional reforms and aggressive enforcement actions that together appear to be reducing the extent of bribery and changing society's overall expectations and tolerance for corruption. Turkey also appears to be tackling corruption successfully through a wide variety of policy and institutional reforms, including a strengthened supreme audit institution and a law on "Freedom of Information for Citizens" enacted in 2003 that has led to a major expansion in the distribution of information to the public through government websites.

More recently, a small number of the more advanced transition countries have begun to address a more complex set of cross-cutting institutional issues related to lobby reform. Hungary has passed a law regulating the lobbying activities of the parliament, the national government, local governments, and the lobbyists and their clients. Latvia, Lithuania, and Estonia are similarly addressing this difficult issue. A glance at recent newspaper headlines in the United States demonstrates the challenges of finding the right balance between the need for a productive dialogue between lawmakers and firms and the unproductive opportunities for corruption that can accompany such dialogue.

The time-series nature of the data collected by Dorhoi (2005) makes it possible to examine how cross-cutting institutions affect the patterns of corruption in subsequent years, and how long it takes for changes in institutions to be reflected in changes in corruption outcomes. Noting that some reform measures more directly control one branch of government than others, Dorhoi groups them into indexes for the executive, the legislature, and the judiciary. Interestingly, the levels of corruption in 2005, as reported by firms, are in some cases more closely correlated with the institutions that existed in 1995 than with those adopted more

---

Box 4.4 Evolution of asset monitoring in Romania

Romania's experience with asset monitoring can best be described as evolutionary. A great stride forward came in 2003 when the government adopted a comprehensive package of laws that included provisions for the public declarations of assets and income. The forms themselves were abysmal: They lacked detail and consisted of simple boxes to check indicating whether or not the official has any assets in the category; the thresholds for many categories were very high (€10,000); and many types of assets did not need to be declared. But they did have the single most important feature of asset declarations—they were public information, posted on the web for high-level officials. The other shortcomings have been redressed in a series of amendments to the law, most recently in January 2005, and the declaration form is now among the most detailed and comprehensive in Europe.

Despite the lack of a formal institution for auditing the declarations, their public nature has made them effective. Prior to the elections in 2004, a group of NGOs, think tanks, and journalists formed a Coalition for a Clean Parliament and created lists of candidates that they viewed as unfit for office. Many criteria were used, including involvement with the Securitate and tax arrears to the budget. Among the key sources of information used to compile the list were the public declarations of assets and income. The Coalition ultimately had an effect on the elections in the fall of 2004, as many candidates were dropped from party lists and there was ultimately a change in the ruling party.

A second stride forward came in early 2005 when the new government, as one of their first major reforms, mandated declarations according to even stricter forms. Now among the toughest in Europe, the new forms call for considerably more detail than the previous version, making it easier for observers (including the general public) to identify discrepancies. The declarations have taken on even greater significance more recently, with several former high-level officials (including a former prime minister) being accused of corruption because of information included in their declarations.

Many challenges remain. While the public nature of the declarations has helped to bring some accountability through the political system, the lack of a workable formal enforcement mechanism means that official sanctions are weak or nonexistent. Plans are currently underway to strengthen enforcement through the creation of a new governmental body whose purpose is to receive and audit the declarations.

See: Romanian Coalition for a Clean Parliament (2005).

recently, indicating that it may take significant time for institutions to change. While recent controls over the executive (that is, those in existence as of 2003) are associated with less frequent bribery, controls related to the other two branches of government that were in existence a decade ago are surprisingly strong predictors of bribe frequency in 2005. A glance at Figure 4.13, which shows the index of controls over legislators in 1995 against the level of bribe frequency in 2005, may give the impression that this is merely a result of the relatively higher levels of income in countries such as Slovenia and Estonia.[23] Indeed, income levels contribute to this pattern, but they do not explain it entirely: Even after controlling for level of income, the pattern apparent in Figure 4.13 remains very strong. Most remarkable is the fact that these two simple variables from a decade ago—controls over legislators and average income—explain 71 percent of the variation in bribe frequency for these 15 countries.

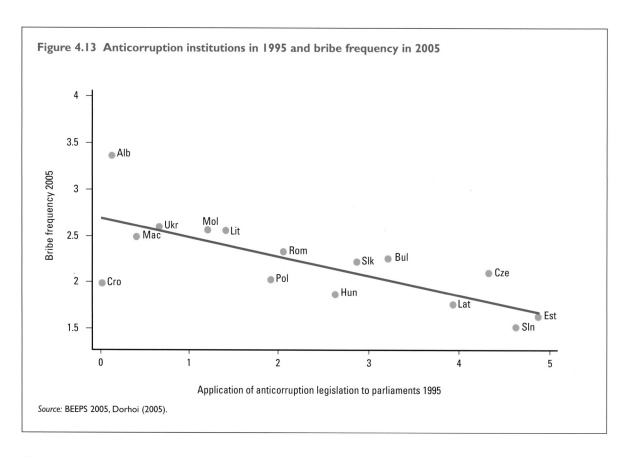

Figure 4.13 Anticorruption institutions in 1995 and bribe frequency in 2005

Source: BEEPS 2005, Dorhoi (2005).

The relationship depicted in Figure 4.13 may well be spurious in the sense that controls over legislators in 1995 can hardly be expected to have a direct link on the propensity of a line inspector to take bribes in 2005. The point is rather that countries that had stronger controls over legislators in 1995, a time when corruption was not as prominent an issue, may have had stronger institutional structures for constraining corruption, and perhaps less cultural acceptance as well, and these long-term factors continue to influence levels of bribery years later.[24]

While this chapter has discussed sector-specific and cross-cutting reforms separately, the two complement each other to varying degrees.[25] In the case of tax administration, for example, sector-specific policies do not explain levels of corruption (in a statistical sense) as well as an index of cross-cutting measures—and both are dominated by the level of income in the country. This stands in contrast to the judiciary, for which sector-specific policies explain much and cross-cutting policies (and income) explain little. Customs and business licensing seem to be influenced in equal measures by cross-cutting and sector-specific policies.

Grouping countries by patterns of corruption

The BEEPS data provide interesting insights into how per capita income levels and other broad legacies of history shape today's patterns of corruption. As noted in Chapter 3, wealthier countries tend to have better institutions and lower levels of firm-level bribery, although there is not clear evidence that rapid economic growth reduces corruption in the short run. Figure 4.14 shows the relationship between (i) levels and changes in per capita income and (ii) levels and changes in corruption by plotting subregional averages of six sector-specific corruption measures against the log of GDP per capita for both 2002 and 2005.[26] While the patterns with regard to taxes, customs, and fire and building inspections are all in the right direction, and the pattern for business licensing is in the right direction for some subregions, those with regard to courts and government procurement are not. With regard to these areas, which face perhaps the most complicated and challenging sets of institutional reforms, there is no "virtuous circle" of higher income leading to lower corruption.

A notable feature of the charts in Figure 4.14 is that subregions do not fit neatly in the sector specific patterns.[27] Southeast Europe stands out for

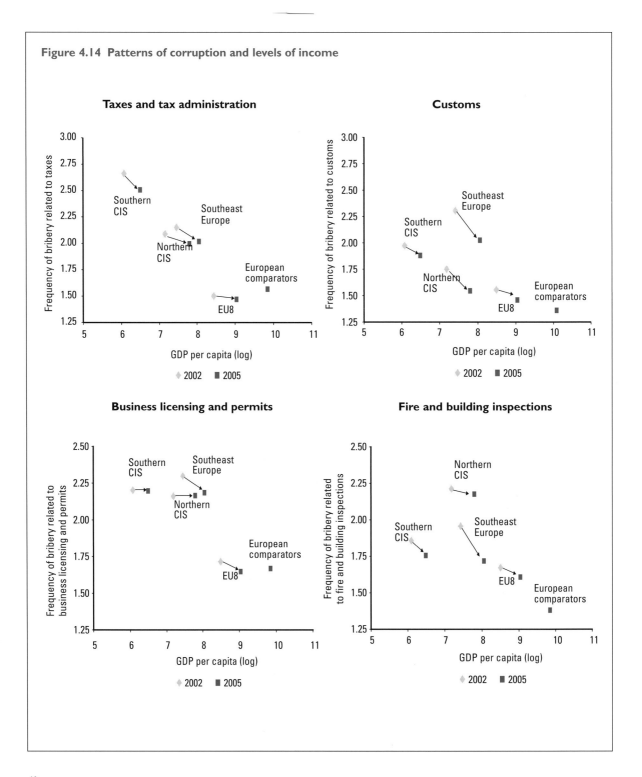

Figure 4.14 Patterns of corruption and levels of income

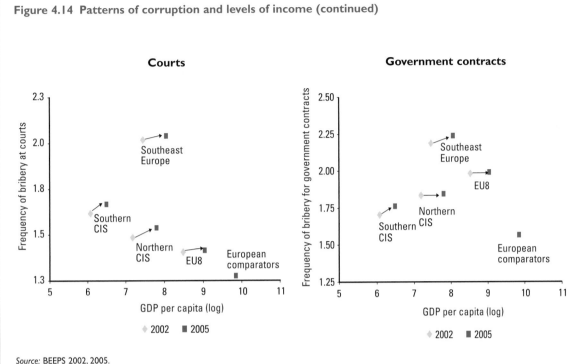

Figure 4.14 Patterns of corruption and levels of income (continued)

Source: BEEPS 2002, 2005.
Note: Southern CIS includes Arm, Aze, Geo, Kyr, Mol, Taj, Uzb; Northern CIS includes Bel, Kaz, Rus, Ukr; Southeast Europe includes Alb, BiH, Bul, Mac, Rom, SAM; EU8 includes Cze, Est, Hun, Lat, Lit, Pol, Slk, Sln; European Comparators include Ger, Gre, Ire, Por, Esp, and Tur. Income levels based on previous full year (2001 and 2004).

customs and the courts; the northern CIS countries are the highest for fire and building inspections; the southern CIS group fares the worst on taxes and tax administration; and firms in the EU-8 report relatively high frequency of bribes with regard to government contracts. Although it is certainly true that subregional groupings do not necessarily reflect the experience of every country in the group, such groupings are typically used to help draw out lessons that may be obscured by the abundance of data. In studies such as this one, it is common to present data according to subgroups such as those in Figure 4.14, and then examine how patterns compare across groups.

Indeed, when it comes to the pattern of corruption, as opposed to the levels, traditional subregional groupings such as those used in Figure 4.14 make sense. Using several variations of cluster analysis, we examined how countries naturally group together, notwithstanding their proximity, history, or other traditional criteria for grouping countries. A full explanation is provided in the Annex, but the essence of cluster analysis as applied here is to see which countries are most similar to each other in terms of the *relative* severity of each of 10 different types of corruption. The resulting clusters are presented in a hierarchy in Figure 4.15. These clusters, based entirely on relative prevalence of types of corruption, map very closely to traditional groupings. One group maps perfectly to the northern CIS, while another covers the Baltics and the Czech and Slovak Republics. Another group is made up entirely of countries of the southern CIS, although Azerbaijan is grouped together with three central Asian countries. Croatia is grouped with Slovenia, and Poland with Hungary. Three of the countries closest to EU accession (Bulgaria, Romania, and FYR Macedonia) are grouped together, and Bosnia and Herzegovina and Serbia and Montenegro form a group. Albania, the country that was perhaps the most isolated for nearly 40 years, has patterns of corruption distinct enough from other countries that it forms its own group.

Figure 4.15 also shows the relative patterns of bribery for each of the groups depicted in the chart. The group that maps exactly to the four countries of the northern CIS has relatively high values for fire and building inspections and business licensing, and relatively lower values for customs and the courts. This does not mean that the levels of corruption in these sectors are low for these countries, just that these forms of corruption were reported to be less prevalent than other forms of corruption. In contrast, all of the fully European groups have relatively greater severity of corruption in procurement, with slight variations in other areas. The groups covering southeast European countries tend to have relatively more trouble with business licensing than the rest of Europe. The group covering Armenia, Georgia, and Moldova has relatively more frequent bribes for business licensing and taxes, while the importance of bribery in tax administration is relatively most acute in the group consisting of Azerbaijan, Tajikistan, Uzbekistan, and the Kyrgyz Republic. Finally, the relative patterns in Albania are notable for both prevalence of bribes at customs and the (relative) lack of bribes for key inspections.[28]

Expanding the analysis to include the six nontransition European countries provides additional insights. Four of the six comparators—Ireland, Turkey, Spain, and Portugal—are most similar to Croatia and Slovenia. Germany, with the relatively high reports of corruption in procurement, is grouped together with the remainder of the EU-8—perhaps not surprising considering that half of the German sample came

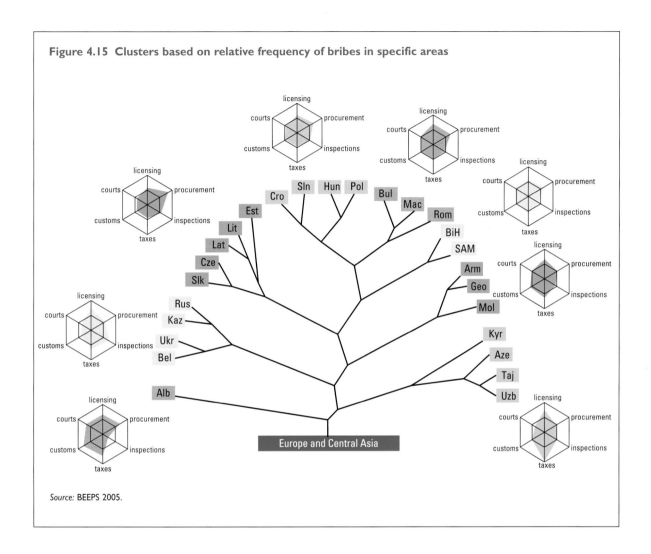

Figure 4.15 Clusters based on relative frequency of bribes in specific areas

Source: BEEPS 2005.

from the former German Democratic Republic. Greece, somewhat surprisingly, is grouped together with Azerbaijan and three central Asian republics, the group where corruption is highest in tax administration.

It is notable that with regard to overall levels of corruption—as measured by overall bribe frequency, bribe tax, and assessments of corruption as a problem doing business—the groupings derived from the data (that is, those that emerge from cluster analysis) bear little resemblance to traditional groupings. This is the main reason that Chapter 2 focuses primarily on individual country measures rather than subregional averages. With regard to specific types of corruption, in contrast, the data suggest groupings that have tremendous overlap with the groups traditionally used, as discussed above.

Several implications derive from these results. First, the long arm of history is clearly present in the data. Countries with similar histories tend to have similar institutions, and the structure of these institutions continues to influence the patterns of corruption. Second, the fact that the comparator countries formed a nearly distinct group suggests that there remain, after all, important differences between even advanced transition countries and elsewhere in Europe. Indeed, it is telling that the two transition countries most closely grouped with the comparator countries are Croatia and Slovenia, as Yugoslavia had perhaps the longest experience with market forces. Finally, it is noteworthy that the richer transition and comparator countries tend to have relatively fewer problems with day-to-day administrative corruption (for example, in tax and customs administration) but relatively higher frequency of bribery in government procurement. This may suggest a typical sequencing over time, whereby countries first gain the capacity to control lower-level administrative corruption as their economies and institutional capacities grow, but continue to have difficulty addressing areas (such as public procurement) that span the boundaries between administrative corruption and state capture. Indeed, corruption scandals in OECD countries often involve bribes paid to politicians to influence large government contracts.

Summary

This chapter looked at specific policy reforms and their impact on corruption in particular areas in transition countries. The extensive policy and administrative reforms that have been undertaken in some areas—most notably taxation, customs, and business licensing and inspections— appear to be having a positive impact in reducing corruption in those areas in many countries. In contrast, less progress is evident in addressing corruption in the judiciary and public procurement, and the impact of cross-cutting measures (such as asset declarations, conflict of interest rules, and anticorruption strategies) is mixed and depends on the extent and seriousness of implementation.

The importance of implementation is also evident throughout this chapter. While the simple relationships depicted in the diagrams are statistically significant, there is considerable deviation for many countries, reflecting, in part, differences in the details of implementation.[29] Indeed, a key difference in terms of both policy and corruption outcomes among three countries that had revolutions during the 2003–2005 period was that Georgia exhibited stronger and more dedicated follow-through and implementation than either Ukraine or the Kyrgyz Republic.

Finally, evidence shows that fundamental change takes time. Despite divergent experiences among countries over the past few years, the long arm of history continues to influence patterns of corruption across the region. Countries with similar histories continue to display similar patterns of corruption, and patterns in transition countries continue to be distinct from those in most comparator European countries further west. Moreover, progress in addressing corruption may proceed in a predictable sequence as countries grow in income and institutional capacity. Richer countries appear to be better able to control low-level administrative corruption but still struggle with forms of corruption—such as bribery in public procurement—that are more likely to be linked to politics and state capture.

Notes

1. Each country received an equal weight in calculating these averages.

2. This section focuses on the prevalence of practices. Thus, "state capture" refers to the prevalence of the practice, not to the impact.

3. In every case, the difference between transition and comparator countries in Figure 4.1 is highly significant. The differences between 2002 and 2005 are all highly significant with the exception of: government contracts ($p = 0.18$), courts ($p = 0.24$), and influence laws ($p = 0.81$).

4. If countries adopt policy reforms in response to pressing problems, and if those reforms take time to work, then the true effectiveness of the policies would be understated by the cross-sectional patterns. As will be seen later in the chapter, some of the cross-cutting policies do seem to take time to work. In contrast, if policy reforms are undertaken in places where they are most likely to be easily implemented, and if these places also have less corruption, then the apparent relationship between policies and corruption outcomes might be overstated. Although it is beyond the scope of this report to fully sort out these complexities, the Annex includes information on a series of simple regressions reflecting the information in the chart, including regressions controlling for level of income. To the extent that income captures many confounding influ-

ences, the patterns that remain after controlling for level of income are more robust than simple correlations. The Annex also explores the use of instrumental variables to limit the impact of endogeneity. Nevertheless, alternative interpretations of the patterns evident in the scatter plots exist—indeed, future explorations of alternative explanations for these observed patterns will add to our understanding of the links between policies and corruption outcomes.

5. Indeed, of the three Doing Business indicators related to taxes, the one that is most closely correlated with levels of corruption is the number of payments per year. As each payment has the potential for both a firm and an inspector to benefit by trading lower taxes for bribes, limiting the number of such interactions reduces the opportunities for corruption.

6. World Bank 2006b.

7. Ades and Di Tella (1999); Treisman (2000).

8. World Bank (2005b).

9. Anderson and Gray (forthcoming).

10. Grodeland (2005) conducted 360 in-depth interviews of elites, including judges and prosecutors, in Bulgaria, the Czech Republic, Romania, and Slovenia and found that expectations of the general public that they would be able to influence judicial proceedings hampered efforts to reform the judiciaries. Grodeland argues that efforts to improve judiciaries should be accompanied by efforts to educate the public in the rule of law.

11. Anderson, Bernstein, and Gray (2005).

12. The World Bank engages in a considerable amount of public procurement, but this is not the focus of the current study. For more information on the World Bank's procurement practices, as well as a list of debarred firms and individuals, see the World Bank's website (http://www.worldbank.org/).

13. The lack of systematic indicators related to public procurement makes it difficult to analyze the relationship between procurement policies and corruption outcomes (Evenett and Hoekman 2005).

14. The average time tax (with each country receiving an equal weight) was 7.5 percent of senior manager's time in 2002 and 5.5 percent in 2005.

15. The focus on civil service is bolstered by research showing that corruption is lower where civil service systems are more meritocratic. Papers by Rauch (2001) and Rauch and Evans (2000) look at meritocracy in a cross-section of countries, and World Bank (2003) also finds meritocracy important for explaining variations in corruption within countries.

16. Hameed (2005) generates an index of fiscal transparency and shows it to be correlated with Transparency International's Corruption Percep-

tions Index. Hameed's measure is also correlated with each of the four main measures of corruption provided by the BEEPS. Countries with higher indexes of fiscal transparency—medium-term budgeting, disclosure of fiscal risks, data quality control, and so forth—tend to have lower levels of corruption.

17. Most studies of the causes of corruption have not examined anticorruption policies or institutions, preferring instead to look at broad measures of institutional quality, usually as assessed by foreign experts. For example, Daniel Treisman's (2000) comprehensive study of the causes of corruption includes measures for openness to trade, resources endowments, and colonial heritage, among others, all very broadly defined. His conclusion that "the distant past appears as important as—or more important than—current policy" may well be true, but the effect of current policy remains an issue.

18. One limitation of this form of research is that there are far more explanatory variables than there are observations. In each of these studies the basic regressions have a large number of correlated right-hand-side variables: 12 explanatory variables for only 24 countries for the original study, and 7 for 26 countries for the update. With regard to the lack of importance of anticorruption strategies, there is an alternative interpretation: Often legislative reforms are enacted only because there was an organizing framework in which the government promised to pass those laws. Isolating the effects of one from the other is not easily achieved by putting both on the right-hand side of a regression.

19. The countries include: Albania, Bulgaria, Croatia, the Czech Republic, Estonia, Hungary, Latvia, Lithuania, FYR Macedonia, Moldova, Poland, Romania, the Slovak Republic, Slovenia, and Ukraine. The nine policy areas include anticorruption strategy (such as general oversight, coordination, and monitoring of progress of anticorruption efforts), anticorruption policy (that is, the main anticorruption agency), political party financing, conflict of interests, asset disclosure, financial control and audit, freedom of information, public procurement, and immunity. The legislation was evaluated qualitatively, and quantitative measurements were then derived.

20. No system will ever be perfect, so a score of "10" does not imply the lack of imperfections. Rather it implies that the law includes all of a certain number of discrete features associated with a quality system.

21. Dorhoi (2005) found that many reform efforts were strong in one area yet weak in another. For example, in countries where assets declarations were fairly comprehensive in terms of disclosure, they may not refer to spouses; if they did refer to spouses, they tended not be comprehensive. In countries where the assets declarations were comprehensive and did cover spouses, the mechanism of enforcement was weak or missing.

22. Like Romania, Albania has also had declarations of assets for several years, and they were publicly released for cabinet members in 2003. Following a strong negative reaction from many officials, however, the manner of publication changed—interested parties had to request the declarations. Many declarations continued to be published by the media, and there are still reports of citizen complaints that certain officials' declarations are false or that certain officials appear to have amassed wealth very quickly. During the elections in June-July 2005, some ministerial-level officials were defeated because of questions surrounding their declarations. Yet the fact that the declarations must be formally requested constrains the ability of the general public to identify discrepancies. See the website of the High Inspectorate for the Declaration and Audit of Assets (http://www.hidaa.gov.al/en/declaration .htm [3/9/2006]).

23. The pattern depicted in Figure 4.13 is the most dramatic ($p = 0.0001$), but there are also significant relationships for other sets of 1995 institutions and 2005 corruption. Controls over legislators in 1995 are significant for explaining state capture in 2005 ($p = 0.07$). Controls over the executive in 1995 are weakly significant for explaining bribe frequency in 2005 ($p = 0.13$). Controls over the judiciary in 1995 are weakly significant for explaining the frequency of bribery in the judiciary in 2005 ($p = 0.09$).

24. Indeed, the application of anticorruption legislation to parliaments in 1995 has no discernible relationship with firms' assessments of bribe-taking by parliamentarians in the 1999 round of the BEEPS. As described in the text, the point of Figure 4.13 is not that the specific policies in existence in 1995 are controlling corruption in 2005, but that the policies in existence in 1995 reflect other factors.

25. Spector, Johnston, and Dininio (2005) argue that sector-specific interventions are more likely to take hold in the long run.

26. As a cardinal measure, GDP per capita is included in log form, while the corruption measures are based on the simple mean from the ordinal scale.

27. If both corruption levels and institutions are determined by level of income, it may be that income is driving the results that are apparent in some of the scatter plots in this chapter. The results vary: In the case of tax administration (Figure 4.3), the effect completely disappears when controlling for level of income. This is due to the very high degree of correlation between the Doing Business measure of ease of paying taxes and the level of income, reinforcing the observation that some elements of tax reform, especially IT-intensive aspects, are expensive. The patterns with regard to business licensing (Figure 4.10) and customs (Figure 4.5) weaken when controlling for level of income, but some rela-

tionship is still evident, and the pattern for courts (Figure 4.7) remains very strong when controlling for level of income. See the Annex for details.

28. As described in the Annex, hierarchical clustering is an iterative process where countries are linked to other countries, and subsequently to other groups of countries, based on how similar they are with respect to the relative frequency of 10 different types of bribes. The small figures show the relative severity of six different types of bribes. "Inspections" in this case refers to fire and building inspections.

29. In addition to variation in strength of implementation, the deviations can also be explained by measurement error and other factors.

5

Closing Thoughts

Corruption is now getting the attention it deserves, not just in rhetoric but in actions as well. By getting detailed information periodically from firms, the BEEPS is helping to monitor progress. At the broadest level, the progress is more encouraging than ever. Firms in many transition countries are reporting that corruption is less frequent, less of a drain on resources, and less of a problem than in the past. Chapter 2 examined four summary indicators of corruption for the period 2002–2005. Not a single country showed deterioration on all four, while numerous countries showed improvement on all of them. Even for the detailed questions about specific types of enterprise-state interactions, most countries showed improvement for most of these indicators, as shown in Chapter 4.

What explains the success achieved to date in some countries in Europe and Central Asia? The data and the evidence both reinforce the fact that rapid progress can be made through the appropriate design and determined implementation of reforms in policies and institutions. The policies that work best are those that simplify rules and regulations, limit interactions between firms and public officials, and reduce burdens on the private sector. Efforts to increase transparency and carefully monitor progress—for example, with the measurement of border crossing times noted in Chapter 4—are powerful tools to highlight remaining areas of corruption and address them. Of course there will always to be an important role for the state, and it is not possible to eliminate all interactions between the public and private sectors. The challenge is rather to think carefully about the governance implications of public policies and to try to minimize opportunities and incentives for corruption wherever feasible.

The trend is favorable but by no means irreversible. Corruption never goes away completely, and even the world's most advanced countries must be constantly on the watch (see Box 5.1). Continued progress in transition countries will require persistent attention to weaknesses and to new challenges as they arise. While many countries have made considerable progress with regard to taxes, customs, and inspections, little if any progress is evident in the judiciary or in public procurement. Usage of the courts and needs for public procurement are both likely to expand with economic growth, and thus the need to address these weaknesses is clear.

An important driver for many countries has been external—most notably the goal of joining the European Union (see Box 5.2). For countries in central and southeast Europe and the Baltics, the EU has provided both the "carrot" of actual or potential membership and the "stick" of conditions and standards, particularly with regard to governance. The EU has also provided technical assistance and regular monitoring of performance. The accession process has had a major

---

Box 5.1 Monitoring corruption and anticorruption in countries at all levels of development

For the past few years the Council of Europe has engaged member countries in a process of peer review of each other's anticorruption legislation and implementation through its "Group of States Against Corruption" (GRECO). These evaluations, which cover many transition countries and all of the BEEPS comparator countries, underscore the fact that all countries encounter corruption and must be constantly vigilant in addressing it. For example, GRECO's review advises Spain to develop better legislation on conflicts of interest. Ireland needs to revise its freedom of information legislation, devote more resources to the detection of corruption, and increase sanctions in corruption cases. Germany is thought to have controlled corruption quite successfully during the privatization and reconstruction process in eastern Germany, but it still needs to address potential conflicts of interest and strengthen its rules on freedom of information.

Greece and Portugal have been highlighted by GRECO—as in the BEEPS—as countries with significant ongoing problems of corruption. Bribery in Portugal is thought to be particularly prevalent at the local level and in certain key central government agencies (including the police, tax administration, and the judiciary, as well as in sports). The evaluation recommends reforms in criminal procedure rules and in immunities given to members of parliament. In Greece, corruption is considered to be significant in public hospitals, the police, tax administration, and the judiciary. Stronger legislation and implementation is thought to be needed in numerous areas, including whistleblower protection, anti-money laundering, ethics rules, and confiscations of proceeds in corruption cases.

For further information, see GRECO reports available at http://www.greco.coe.int/.

Box 5.2 The pull of the European Union

Data reinforce the view that EU membership has provided a major incentive for countries in Central and Eastern Europe to address corruption. Figure 5.1 shows the intensity of anticorruption legislation in two periods—1995–2002 and 2002–2003—for 15 countries in various stages of EU accession. The first group covers the first "wave" of five accession countries, while the second group covers the three countries that were originally referred to as the second wave but subsequently merged with the first wave. The third group covers Bulgaria and Romania, two countries expected to join the EU in 2007 or 2008 (depending on progress), and the fourth includes Croatia and FYR Macedonia, two of the three current candidate countries. The final group includes Albania, Moldova, and Ukraine, European countries that would like to join the EU in the future but are not currently candidates. As is evident, anticorruption activity was most pronounced for countries whose accession was probable but not certain—the second wave of countries in 1995–2002 and the third and fourth waves in 2002–2003.

Figure 5.1 Anticorruption intensity and the pull of the European Union

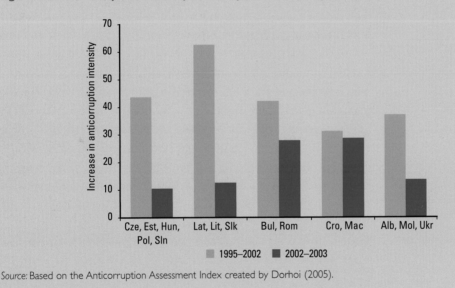

Source: Based on the Anticorruption Assessment Index created by Dorhoi (2005).

impact in stimulating recent anticorruption efforts in Romania and Bulgaria and is likely to have a similar impact in many other countries in the region. Indeed, the desire to meet European standards is a motivator for governance improvements far beyond the borders of the EU.

This study also underlines the importance of a country's political system as either a driver or inhibitor of reform. The political system inevitably defines the incentives and sets the boundaries within which policies and institutions are formed. Chapter 3 discussed the fact that countries with less open and competitive political and economic regimes tend to have more moderate indicators of corruption as reported by firms. These survey outcomes could reflect the strong control environment, the low level of private-sector activity, different conceptions of what constitutes corruption, or the hesitation of respondents to answer questions freely. But no matter the reason, it is clear that technocratic reforms are not likely to have the same effect in closed environments. Without a substantial move toward greater openness and transparency, these countries are unlikely to make real progress in improving public-sector accountability and performance. It is possible that the opening up of closed political systems will lead to higher corruption in the short term, but over time more political and economic competition helps foster the transparency and accountability that is essential in controlling corruption.

Finally, individuals matter, and strong leadership is essential in shaping and pushing reform.[1] Every country that has achieved some success on the anticorruption front has had leaders who have tenaciously pushed the reform agenda. Romanian leaders strengthened the asset declaration law immediately upon taking office and have worked to support prosecutors who are also keen to tackle corruption. Slovak leaders have been instrumental in pursuing far-reaching tax and budget reforms. The Georgian government has doggedly pursued fundamental reforms in many areas since the Rose Revolution in late 2003. On the other hand, a lesson from countries with less success to date is that reforms will not achieve the desired results unless there is real support from the leadership and a strong push on implementation. Leaders cannot expect to eliminate corruption, but the experience of the countries of Europe and Central Asia shows that those with strong commitment, courage, and support can make an important difference in a relatively short period of time.

Note

1. "Political will" has for years been cited as key for reducing corruption, almost to the point of cliché. Nevertheless, the importance of political will remains as unmistakable as it is difficult to analyze. A recent study used a novel approach to test assertions about what factors help generate success in anticorruption interventions. Employing a meta-analysis of 35 case studies, Spector, Johnston, and Dininio (2005) find that political will is key for making reforms sustainable. Interestingly, they also find that while anticorruption programs are less likely to be successful under generally worsening economic and social conditions, they tend to be more successful under crisis conditions "when leaders and the general public may be jolted into seeking fixes that will resolve the crisis..." (p. 222).

Methodological Annex

T his Annex describes in more depth some issues of methodology, as well as analytical results underpinning some of the conclusions in the text.

BEEPS survey questions

Bribe frequency:

Thinking about officials, would you say the following statements are always, usually, frequently, sometimes, seldom, or never true?
   (Never=1 Seldom=2 Sometimes=3 Frequently=4 Usually=5 Always=6)
"It is common for firms in my line of business to have to pay some irregular 'additional payments/gifts' to get things done with regard to customs, taxes, licenses, regulations, services etc."

Bribe tax

On average, what percent of total annual sales do firms like yours typically pay in unofficial payments/gifts to public officials? _____%

Kickback Tax

When firms in your industry do business with the government, what percent of the contract value would be typically paid in additional or unofficial payments/gifts to secure the contract? _____%

Corruption as a problem doing business

Can you tell me how problematic are these different factors for the operation and growth of your business: ... Corruption
    (No obstacle=1 Minor obstacle=2 Moderate obstacle=3 Major obstacle=4)

Sector-specific bribe frequency

Thinking now of unofficial payments/gifts that a firm like yours would make in a given year, could you please tell me how often would they make payments/gifts for the following purposes:
    (Never=1 Seldom=2 Sometimes=3 Frequently=4 Usually=5 Always=6)

- To get connected to and maintain public services (electricity and telephone)
- To obtain business licenses and permits
- To obtain government contracts
- To deal with occupational health and safety inspections
- To deal with fire and building inspections
- To deal with environmental inspections
- To deal with taxes and tax collection
- To deal with customs/imports
- To deal with courts
- To influence the content of new legislation rules decrees etc.

State capture

It is often said that firms make unofficial payments/gifts, private payments, or other benefits to public officials to gain advantages in the drafting of laws, decrees, regulations, and other binding government decisions. To what extent have the following practices had a direct impact on your business.
    (No impact=0 Minor impact=1 Moderate impact=2 Major impact=3 Decisive impact=4)

- Private payments/gifts or other benefits to parliamentarians to affect their votes
- Private payments/gifts or other benefits to government officials to affect the content of government decrees

Notes on statistical significance

The many charts in this report that show changes over time for individual countries include mention below the chart of which changes are statistically significant changes. These determinations were based on simple *t*-tests for difference in means, and the threshold was set for a *p*-value of 10 percent. It should also be noted that when comparing values for different countries, those near each other on the charts are often not significantly different. For example, in Figure 2.1, the percentage of firms that said corruption was a problem in Albania in 2005 is not significantly different from the 2005 value for the Kyrgyz Republic, but it is significantly higher than the 2005 value for FYR Macedonia and other countries.

Sensitivity to treatment of nonresponse and possible respondent reticence

Throughout the report we have presented simple averages over all non-missing observations, standard practice for such reports. Comparing 2002 to 2005, there was some increase in the percentage of firms that did not answer the relevant questions for one reason or another. For bribe frequency, for example, there was an increase in missing values, from 7.1 to 10.9 percent.[1] There were also increases in the percentage of missing values for the bribe tax (from 8.8 to 12.0 percent), for parliament capture (from 14.6 to 16.7 percent), and for executive decree capture (from 14.7 to 17.0 percent). For corruption as a problem doing business, there was a slight decrease in missing values, from 6.8 to 6.3 percent.

To test the sensitivity of the main corruption measures used in this report to assumptions about the meaning of nonresponses and concerns about respondent candidness, we constructed four alternative variations of each of the three corruption measures. An explanation of the alternative assumptions, and the correlation of the resulting measure with the unadjusted measure, are provided in Table 1. For every scenario, the resulting values are highly correlated with the simple measure.

While the overall results are not sensitive to alternative assumptions about reticence and nonresponse, some of the individual country trends are influenced due to large changes in the incidence of nonresponse in some countries. Applying the (rather extreme) alternative assumptions

Table 1 Sensitivity to assumptions about reticence and nonresponse

Correlations between the level in 2005 and the level under the alternative scenarios; and between the change between 2002 and 2005 and the change under the alternative scenarios		Corruption as a problem	Bribe tax	Bribe frequency
Restrict the sample to firms that complained about at least one aspect of the business environment in the "problems doing business" question. This had the largest effects on Uzbekistan (9% sample reduction), Estonia (8%), Armenia (7%), and Turkey (7%).	Level in 2005	0.998	0.999	0.999
	Change between 2002 and 2005	0.992	0.996	0.997
Restrict the sample to firms that gave a nonzero response to at least one of the questions about corruption. This had the largest effects on Uzbekistan (9% sample reduction), Serbia and Montenegro (5%), Bosnia and Herzegovina (5%), and Poland (5%).	Level in 2005	0.957	0.981	0.971
	Change between 2002 and 2005	0.930	0.954	0.955
Assume that missing responses indicate a lack of knowledge about the corrupt activity in the question, and set them equal to the value indicating "no corruption."	Level in 2005	0.994	0.977	0.988
	Change between 2002 and 2005	0.992	0.964	0.975
Assume that missing responses indicate that the firm has knowledge about the corrupt activity and just doesn't want to reveal it, and set these missing responses equal to the average of the positive responses for that country and that year.	Level in 2005	0.987	0.941	0.990
	Change between 2002 and 2005	0.983	0.924	0.981

presented in Table 1 to individual countries, we tested whether the trends that are apparent in the simple charts throughout this report might be affected. Done for five measures of corruption, four alternative assumptions, and 26/7 countries, this comes to 536 different trends, of which 40 would reverse under an alternative assumption. The overwhelming majority of these are countries/measures that had little change to begin with. Of the country/measures where the change in the simple measure is statistically significant at the 10 percent level, there were only four cases of reversal under an extreme assumption: Turkey's improvement on bribe frequency, Georgia's improvement in parliamentary and executive decree capture, and Belarus' improvement in executive decree capture would all vanish with the assumption that every single one of the "missings" is really a positive response. For corruption as a problem and the bribe tax, no country that shows a significant change would experience a sign reversal under any of the alternative scenarios.

Note that the extreme assumption described above assigns every one of the missing values the rating of the average of the nonzero, nonmissing responses. This assumes, for example, that not even one firm in the sample truly did not know whether they are affected by parliamentary capture. This test only examined whether a statistically significant change would vanish—that is, the sign would change—not whether it would decline in level of significance. Given that the alternative assumptions are extreme and implausible, constructed only for the purpose of sensitivity testing, this was appropriate.

Sensitivity to respondent optimism

Following the methodology laid out in World Bank (2004), a rudimentary index of respondent "optimism" was constructed to account for the fact that some respondents tend to give uniformly positive responses and others give uniformly negative responses, even when they are describing the same thing. The methodology for constructing the "optimism" variable focuses on complaints about macroeconomic conditions (inflation and exchange rate volatility), a variable that would tend to have relatively little firm-specific incidence. Firms that complained relatively more about macroeconomic uncertainty than would be predicted based on actual inflation and exchange rate volatility measures have lower values for "optimism," and those that complained relatively little had higher values for optimism.

A simple test was conducted to explore the sensitivity to firm-level optimism of the country-specific trends described in the text for the four main corruption measures. While the notes on statistical significance in the figures are based on simple t-tests, the additional test involved a regression of the corruption measure on the optimism measure and a dummy for the survey year, checking to see if the coefficient on the dummy variable maintains the same sign even after controlling for firm-level optimism. For the four main measures of corruption, for 27 countries, there were only four instances where the direction of the trend changed after controlling for respondent optimism: Serbia and Montenegro for both bribe frequency and corruption as a problem doing business, and Kazakhstan and Romania for corruption as a problem doing business.

Sensitivity to sample selection

Sampling in the BEEPS reflected the actual distribution of firms in the countries according to each sector's contribution to GDP, with certain exceptions. Some sectors were excluded, such as farms and regulated industries, and the sampling approach required minimum numbers of firms with certain characteristics, such as exporters, state-owned enterprises, large firms, and so forth. It is not possible to gauge the impact of excluding certain sectors, although it is possible to examine the impact of differences in ex post sample characteristics by weighting the characteristics so that they have the same share of the sample in every country. Focusing on size and sector, the reweighted samples exhibit virtually identical patterns as those depicted in the charts in this report based on simple averages from the overall sample.

While the BEEPS surveys in 2002 and 2005 used a nearly identical approach to sampling, one innovation in sampling may have influenced the results. In particular, the 2005 sample included a number of firms that also participated in the 2002 survey, firms that we refer to as the "panel firms." This innovation to the sample provides a needed longitudinal perspective. However, since a key criteria of sample selection in both years is that the firm be at least three years old—a rule selected so that firm performance over the previous three years could be tracked—the inclusion of the panel firms in 2005 meant that a significant portion of the sample was at least six years old, resulting in an "older" sample in 2005. If newer firms are more beset by corruption, and this does seem to be the case, then some of the apparent reduction in levels of corruption between 2002 and 2005 could be due to this modest innovation in sampling methodology. Indeed, Hallward-Driemeier (2006) found using the same data that the incidence of corruption did have an impact on firm exit.

The impact of the panel sampling would be less of an issue if the overall samples had similar age structures, for example if the 6+ year old panel firms (survivors) merely replaced other 6+ year old firms in the sample (also survivors, by definition).[2] In fact, the sample in 2005 was older than the one in 2002, whether including the panel firms or not. The average firm age in 2002 was 14.7 years, whereas the average ages of panel and nonpanel firms, respectively, were 18.3 and 15.3 years. This is partly explained by the fact that the 2002 survey began slightly later in the spring, and the sampling rule that firms be at least three years old meant that the 2002 sample included some firms that were established three calendar years earlier, whereas all of the firms in the 2005 sample were established at least four calendar years earlier.

As a stronger test of the sensitivity of key results to the panel aspect of the dataset and to the fact that 3-year-old firms were included in 2002 but not 2005, we calculated the averages of the four key indicators of corruption for firms that are more than six years old. The results are presented in Table 2. Restricting the sample to firms more than six years old does not have an appreciable effect on most of the qualitative conclusions generated by the full sample: The magnitudes of the improvements in bribe tax and bribe frequency are somewhat smaller for the restricted

Table 2 Change in key corruption variables when restricting sample to older firms

	Average of country means		Average of country means for firms > 6 years old	
	2002	2005	2002	2005
Corruption as a problem (scale of 1 to 4)	2.24	2.15	2.26	2.13
Bribe tax (percent of revenue)	1.64	1.05	1.49	0.98
Bribe frequency (scale of 1 to 6)	2.61	2.35	2.54	2.32
State capture (scale of 0 to 4)	0.40	0.36	0.40	0.36

sample, while the magnitude of the improvement in corruption as a problem doing business is somewhat larger for the restricted sample. There is no impact on state capture measures.

Regarding the individual country patterns, no country that is marked in the text as having a significant change in any of the four main corruption measures would have a sign reversal by focusing on the restricted sample, although some do have a decline in the level of significance, due partially to the smaller sample sizes. For corruption as a problem, the deteriorations for Azerbaijan and the Kyrgyz Republic are not significant at the 10 percent level when restricting the sample to firms more than six years old. For bribe frequency, the deterioration in the Kyrgyz Republic and the improvements in Latvia, Moldova, and Ukraine are not significant for older firms. For bribe tax, the improvements in Czech Republic, Kazakhstan, Moldova, the Slovak Republic, and Uzbekistan are not significant for older firms. For state capture, the improvements in Latvia and the Slovak Republic fall in significance, and the deteriorations in Albania and Poland are not significant when restricting the sample to firms that are more than six years old.

Regression results and correlations

Chapter 3 reports on the results of regressions that combine firm-level characteristics and country-level measures in a single framework. The methodology and results for 2002 are described in ACT2 (World Bank 2004). The results are shown in Table 3, with the dependent variables listed across the top and the explanatory variables on the left. All regressions allowed for clustering of errors within a country, and robust

Table 3 Regressions on firm characteristics and country level variables, 2005

	Bribe tax (1)	Corruption as a problem (2)	Bribe frequency (3)	State capture (4)	Bribe to influence law (5)	Bribe to get connected (6)	Bribe to get licenses (7)	Bribe for government contracts (8)	Bribe for taxes (9)	Bribe for customs (10)	Bribe for courts (11)
Age	-0.17***	-0.05**	-0.19***	-0.03*	-0.04*	-0.08***	-0.16***	-0.11***	-0.18***	-0.11***	-0.08***
	(0.00)	(0.02)	(0.00)	(0.09)	(0.06)	(0.00)	(0.00)	(0.00)	(0.00)	(0.01)	(0.01)
Small firm	0.25**	-0.04	-0.10	-0.08**	-0.03	0.00	0.01	0.04	-0.01	-0.06	-0.04
	(0.01)	(0.50)	(0.17)	(0.01)	(0.41)	(0.90)	(0.80)	(0.47)	(0.81)	(0.39)	(0.49)
Private	0.36**	0.19***	0.39***	0.00	0.03	-0.01	0.24***	0.21**	0.17	0.19***	0.15**
	(0.01)	(0.00)	(0.00)	(0.93)	(0.56)	(0.89)	(0.01)	(0.02)	(0.03)	(0.01)	(0.05)
Foreign owned	-0.29***	-0.02	-0.17**	-0.02	-0.01	-0.07*	-0.15**	-0.18***	-0.07	0.24**	-0.09*
	(0.01)	(0.59)	(0.03)	(0.58)	(0.89)	(0.08)	(0.02)	(0.00)	(0.36)	(0.01)	(0.09)
Manufacturer	0.26***	0.07*	0.18***	0.00	0.04	0.04	0.12*	0.41***	0.08*	0.14***	0.07*
	(0.01)	(0.07)	(0.00)	(0.92)	(0.14)	(0.14)	(0.02)	(0.00)	(0.07)	(0.00)	(0.07)
City	0.09**	0.02	0.06***	0.02*	0.03**	0.00	0.04**	0.09***	0.03	0.05**	0.04**
	(0.03)	(0.24)	(0.01)	(0.10)	(0.01)	(0.78)	(0.01)	(0.00)	(0.18)	(0.04)	(0.02)
GDP growth	0.02	-0.05**	-0.04	-0.02	-0.01	-0.02	-0.02	-0.04*	-0.04	-0.03	-0.03
	(0.74)	(0.02)	(0.35)	(0.19)	(0.56)	(0.49)	(0.49)	(0.07)	(0.47)	(0.33)	(0.16)
Years in office	0.04	0.00	0.00	-0.01	-0.01	-0.01	0.00	-0.02	0.03	-0.01	-0.01
	(0.32)	(0.77)	(1.00)	(0.13)	(0.38)	(0.39)	(0.80)	(0.20)	(0.40)	(0.81)	(0.59)
Legislative election	-0.26	0.05	-0.19	-0.07	-0.06	-0.13	-0.11	0.08	-0.32	-0.10	-0.18
	(0.12)	(0.72)	(0.33)	(0.19)	(0.35)	(0.18)	(0.34)	(0.38)	(0.14)	(0.41)	(0.11)
CPIA indicator	-0.17	-0.15	-0.54***	-0.09	-0.01	-0.25**	-0.39***	-0.02	-0.44***	-0.26	-0.26*
	(0.33)	(0.15)	(0.01)	(0.14)	(0.92)	(0.03)	(0.00)	(0.86)	(0.04)	(0.12)	(0.05)
Optimism	-0.11*	-0.38***	-0.18***	-0.05***	-0.10***	-0.08**	-0.16***	-0.21***	-0.16***	-0.17***	-0.16***
	(0.06)	(0.00)	(0.00)	(0.00)	(0.00)	(0.01)	(0.00)	(0.00)	(0.00)	(0.00)	(0.00)
Bribe tax		0.09***									
		(0.00)									
Active capture				0.31***							
				(0.00)							
Constant	1.05	3.04***	4.93***	0.59	1.58***	2.85***	3.78***	2.21***	4.06***	2.98***	3.01***
	(0.28)	(0.00)	(0.00)	(0.10)	(0.00)	(0.00)	(0.00)	(0.00)	(0.00)	(0.01)	(0.00)
Observations	5531	5273	5565	4618	5164	5641	5591	5264	5565	5224	5261
Adjusted R-squared	0.03	0.21	0.09	0.18	0.02	0.03	0.06	0.06	0.09	0.05	0.05

Sources: Data constructed from BEEPS 2005; World Bank's Database of Political Institutions; World Bank's CPIA indicators; and World Development Indicators.

Note: Robust *p* values in parentheses: * significant at 10%; ** significant at 5%; *** significant at 1%. Regressions include all ECA countries except for Bosnia and Herzegovina, Slovenia and Uzbekistan, and Turkey for lack of at least one variable.

(heteroskedasticity adjusted) *p*-values are in parentheses. Variable definitions are the same as in ACT2:

Age	Number of years since the firm began operations in that country (logs)
Small firm	Dummy for firms with less than 50 employees
Private	Dummy for privately owned firms
Foreign owned	Dummy for firms that are foreign owned
Manufacturer	Dummy for manufacturing, construction, or mining
City	Population of the city where the firm is located: 1=under 50,000; 2=between 50,000 and 250,000; 3=between 250,000 and 1,000,000; 4=over 1,000,000; 5=capital
GDP growth	Growth rate of GDP, 1 year lag
Years in office	Number of years the chief executive has been in office
Legislative election	Dummy for legislative elections in the previous calendar year (2004)
CPIA indicator	Average of eight CPIA indicators including management of inflation and macroeconomic imbalances; trade policy and foreign exchange regime; competitive environment for the private sector; factor and product markets; quality of public administration; quality of budgetary and financial management; efficiency of revenue mobilization; and property rights and rule-based governance.
Optimism	Residuals of regressing macroeconomic perception ("How problematic macroeconomic instability is for the operation and growth of your business?") on actual levels of inflation and exchange rate volatility and adding dummies for firms that export products and/or import supplies. A higher score represents a more optimistic view while a lower score a more pessimistic view about the macroeconomic conditions.

Chapter 3 also describes the results of regressions based on the panel data. As each firm in the panel dataset responded to the survey in both 2002 and 2005, a measure of the change in assessment could be constructed for each firm. These are the dependent variables, shown across the top of Table 4, with the explanatory variables on the left. All regressions allowed for clustering of errors within a country, and robust (heteroskedasticity adjusted) *p*-values are in parentheses.

Chapter 4 presents scatter plots of measures of corruption outcomes against measures of policy taken from the Doing Business indicators. Table 5 through Table 8 show the results of regressing one on the other, as well as the effects of adding the log of GDP per capita in 2004 and various measures of cross-cutting reforms. Sector-specific measures are

Table 4 Panel regression results

	Change in bribe tax (1)	Change in corruption as a problem (2)	Change in bribe frequency (3)	Change in state capture (4)	Change in active capture (5)
Age	0.35	−0.04	−0.02	−0.03	−0.02
	(0.10)	(0.49)	(0.86)	(0.76)	(0.71)
Small firm	−0.24	−0.01	−0.14	0.05	0.12
	(0.55)	(0.92)	(0.34)	(0.52)	(0.33)
Private	0.16	−0.17	−0.24	−0.07	−0.11
	(0.72)	(0.15)	(0.22)	(0.61)	(0.36)
Foreign owner	0.14	−0.03	−0.03	0.08	0.03
	(0.65)	(0.88)	(0.88)	(0.34)	(0.78)
Manufacturer	0.01	0.07	0.14	0.12**	0.07
	(0.98)	(0.40)	(0.14)	(0.04)	(0.24)
City	−0.01	−0.06	0	0	0.01
	(0.90)	(0.14)	(0.94)	(0.89)	(0.83)
GDP growth	0.1	0.05	0.01	0.01	0.05*
	(0.15)	(0.19)	(0.81)	(0.69)	(0.08)
Average CPIA	0.56**	0.18	−0.06	−0.07	0.09
	(0.04)	(0.21)	(0.74)	(0.44)	(0.35)
Optimism	0.13	−0.22***	−0.12**	−0.08**	0
	(0.27)	(0.00)	(0.05)	(0.02)	(0.96)
Bribe tax		0.03			
		(0.20)			
Active Capture				0.29***	
				(0.00)	
Constant	−4.29***	−0.64	0.27	−0.15	−0.65
	(0.01)	(0.36)	(0.80)	(0.82)	(0.22)
Observations	1027	1024	1054	782	906
Adjusted *R*-squared	0.00	0.04	0.00	0.10	0.00

Note: Robust *p* values in parentheses:
* significant at 10%; ** significant at 5%; *** significant at 1%.

taken from Doing Business and include both specific indicators (such as number of procedures, time, and cost) as well as a summary that is simply the global rank for that area. The Doing Business measures (including the ranks) are higher for countries with more onerous systems, so we would expect positive coefficients. The cross-cutting measures include the index of anticorruption legislation adopted between 1999 and 2002 from Rousso and Steves (2005), the World Bank's CPIA assessment of quality of budget and financial management, and the CPIA assessment of quality of public administration. These are all higher for countries with better systems, so we would expect negative coefficients. The index of cross-cutting institutions was created by a principal components procedure of these three variables. The index is a weighted average of the three, with very nearly equal weights as they each have similar loads on the first principal component.

The regressions presented in Table 5 through Table 8 could arguably be mis-specified if the measures of corruption and of institutions are endogenous. Perhaps, for example, some aspect of history or culture has influenced both the level of corruption and the quality of institutions. The sector-specific proxies taken from Doing Business seem less susceptible to this problem, as many are policy levers that can be reformed relatively quickly. Indeed, many of the Doing Business indicators are not even correlated with each other. The cross-cutting measures, in contrast, would seem to be more susceptible to problems of endogeneity.

Although it is beyond the scope of this report to fully sort out the issues of endogeneity—thus the use of the word "association" in the captions to the tables—efforts were made to explore the robustness of the main results. The regressions that include GDP per capita have already addressed this issue to some extent, as this variable would capture many factors that might be generating endogeneity. For the equations that do not include GDP per capita, and focusing on the ones using the indices of cross-cutting and sector-specific measures, two-stage least squares was employed with instruments for the cross-cutting index. The instruments include: distance from Dusseldorf; years under communism; and secondary school enrollment in 1990, drawing on de Melo, Denizer, Gelb, and Tenev (1997) and Fischer and Sahay (2000). All of the results depicted in column (4) of each of Table 5 through Table 8 are confirmed using this approach.

Chapter 4 also describes cross-cutting anticorruption reforms as reported in Dorhoi (2005). As these were only available for 15 countries, there was limited scope for multivariate regression. Table 9 presents simple correlations between the measures of corruption outcomes and cross-cutting anticorruption policies.

Chapter 4 also describes the results of hierarchical cluster analysis examining how countries naturally group together, notwithstanding their proximity, history, or other traditional criteria for grouping countries. Cluster analysis is an exploratory approach to data analysis, one that does not test hypotheses determined a priori, but rather illuminates underlying structures in the data. Hierarchical clustering separates observations, in this case countries, into a hierarchy of groups based on how similar or dissimilar they appear in the data. This is done through an iterative procedure as in the following example for hierarchical clustering according to ten different variables: First, the Euclidian distance for every pair of countries is computed. The two countries with the smallest distance (that is, those that are the most similar) are then marked as a group. This pair of countries is then treated as if it were a single country, with the variables representing the average of the two countries. The process is then repeated iteratively until there remains only a single group comprised of all countries.

Table 5 Sector-specific and cross-cutting policies: association with tax bribery

| | Dependent variable = bribery for dealing with taxes and tax administration | | | | | | | | |
	(1)	(2)	(3)	(4)	(5)	(6)	(7)	(8)	(9)
Rank for dealing with taxes	0.005			0.001	−0.001				
	(0.14)			(0.83)	(0.65)				
Index of cross-cutting institutions		−0.229		−0.221	−0.042				
		(0.01)***		(0.00)***	(0.67)				
GDP per capita (log)			−0.417		−0.396				−0.502
			(0.00)***		(0.07)*				(0.02)**
Number of tax payments per year						0.011		−0.001	−0.004
						(0.04)**		(0.93)	(0.57)
Time needed to deal with taxes						−0.000		−0.000	−0.000
						(0.52)		(0.68)	(0.18)
Impact of taxes on profits						−0.008		−0.004	0.001
						(0.37)		(0.64)	(0.93)
Quality of budget and financial management							0.085	−0.011	0.264
							(0.77)	(0.97)	(0.39)
Quality of public administration							−0.428	−0.369	−0.006
							(0.14)	(0.25)	(0.98)
Index of anticorruption legislation							−0.477	−0.678	−0.834
							(0.42)	(0.27)	(0.13)
Constant	1.530	2.001	5.273	1.951	5.237	1.866	3.413	3.962	5.697
	(0.00)***	(0.00)***	(0.00)***	(0.00)***	(0.01)***	(0.00)***	(0.00)***	(0.00)***	(0.00)***
Observations	24	24	24	24	24	24	24	24	24
R-squared	0.10	0.32	0.44	0.32	0.45	0.19	0.35	0.37	0.54

Sources: BEEPS 2005, *Doing Business in 2006* (World Bank 2006), World Bank's CPIA 2004, Rousso and Steves (2005) based on anticorruption laws and policies adopted between 1999 and 2002; World Development Indicators for GDP per capita in 2004.

Note: Robust p values in parentheses: * significant at 10%; ** significant at 5%; *** significant at 1%. Regressions include all ECA countries except for Slovenia, Tajikistan, Turkey, and Turkmenistan, for lack of at least one variable.

Table 6 Sector-specific and cross-cutting policies: association with customs bribery

	Dependent variable = bribery for dealing with customs/imports								
	(1)	(2)	(3)	(4)	(5)	(6)	(7)	(8)	(9)
Rank for trading across borders	0.004			0.004	0.003				
	(0.03)**			(0.11)	(0.23)				
Index of cross-cutting institutions		−0.095		−0.026	0.016				
		(0.10)*		(0.68)	(0.81)				
GDP per capita (log)			−0.178		−0.110				−0.298
			(0.03)**		(0.37)				(0.10)
Number of documents needed for imports						0.027		0.030	0.050
						(0.28)		(0.30)	(0.08)*
Number of signatures needed for imports						0.005		0.001	−0.005
						(0.53)		(0.88)	(0.57)
Time needed to deal with import requirements						−0.001		−0.003	−0.007
						(0.90)		(0.62)	(0.24)
Quality of budget and financial management							0.008	−0.083	0.027
							(0.96)	(0.68)	(0.91)
Quality of public administration							−0.309	−0.211	−0.048
							(0.11)	(0.38)	(0.87)
Index of anticorruption legislation							0.268	0.125	0.037
							(0.62)	(0.82)	(0.95)
Constant	1.407	1.766	3.163	1.462	2.393	1.396	2.646	2.503	3.953
	(0.00)***	(0.00)***	(0.00)***	(0.00)***	(0.03)**	(0.00)***	(0.00)***	(0.01)**	(0.00)***
Observations	24	24	24	24	24	24	24	24	24
R-squared	0.16	0.10	0.15	0.16	0.18	0.11	0.16	0.19	0.26

Sources: BEEPS 2005, *Doing Business in 2006* (World Bank 2006), World Bank's CPIA 2004, Rousso and Steves (2005) based on anticorruption laws and policies adopted between 1999 and 2002; World Development Indicators for GDP per capita in 2004.
Notes: Robust *p* values in parentheses: * significant at 10%; ** significant at 5%; *** significant at 1%. Regressions include all ECA countries except for Slovenia, Tajikistan, Turkey, and Turkmenistan, for lack of at least one variable.

Table 7 Sector-specific and cross-cutting policies: association with bribery in courts

	Dependent variable = bribery in courts								
	(1)	(2)	(3)	(4)	(5)	(6)	(7)	(8)	(9)
Rank for enforcing contracts	0.007			0.007	0.007				
	(0.00)***			(0.02)**	(0.03)**				
Index of cross-cutting institutions		−0.081		0.007	0.016				
		(0.11)		(0.91)	(0.82)				
GDP per capita (log)			−0.110		−0.018				0.030
			(0.12)		(0.85)				(0.86)
Number of procedures to enforce a contract						0.014		0.019	0.020
						(0.10)*		(0.09)*	(0.11)
Time to enforce a contract						0.000		−0.000	−0.000
						(0.89)		(0.83)	(0.83)
Cost of enforcing a contract						0.016		0.022	0.023
						(0.03)**		(0.08)*	(0.11)
Quality of budget and financial management							0.015	0.200	0.187
							(0.94)	(0.30)	(0.37)
Quality of public administration							−0.139	0.022	0.002
							(0.48)	(0.90)	(0.99)
Index of anticorruption legislation							−0.178	−0.048	−0.047
							(0.74)	(0.93)	(0.93)
Constant	1.249	1.694	2.556	1.239	1.381	0.963	2.211	−0.069	−0.196
	(0.00)***	(0.00)***	(0.00)***	(0.00)***	(0.11)	(0.00)***	(0.00)***	(0.94)	(0.88)
Observations	24	24	24	24	24	24	24	24	24
R-squared	0.36	0.09	−0.110	0.36	0.36	0.30	0.09	0.34	0.34

Sources: BEEPS 2005, *Doing Business in 2006* (World Bank 2006), World Bank's CPIA 2004, Rousso and Steves (2005) based on anticorruption laws and policies adopted between 1999 and 2002; World Development Indicators for GDP per capita in 2004.

Notes: Robust p values in parentheses: * significant at 10%; ** significant at 5%; *** significant at 1%. Regressions include all ECA countries except for Slovenia, Tajikistan, Turkey, and Turkmenistan, for lack of at least one variable.

Table 8 Sector-specific and cross-cutting policies: association with licensing bribery

	Dependent variable = bribery for dealing with business licensing and permits								
	(1)	(2)	(3)	(4)	(5)	(6)	(7)	(8)	(9)
Rank for dealing with licenses	0.003			0.002	0.002				
	(0.09)*			(0.34)	(0.21)				
Index of cross-cutting institutions		−0.161		−0.147	−0.077				
		(0.00)***		(0.00)***	(0.22)				
GDP per capita (log)			−0.239		−0.134				−0.202
			(0.00)***		(0.20)				(0.17)
Number of procedures for dealing with licenses						−0.004		−0.003	−0.004
						(0.73)		(0.82)	(0.71)
Time to deal with licenses						0.001		0.000	0.001
						(0.25)		(0.75)	(0.36)
Cost of dealing with licenses						0.000		0.000	−0.000
						(0.73)		(1.00)	(0.75)
Quality of budget and financial management							0.113	0.102	0.172
							(0.47)	(0.57)	(0.33)
Quality of public administration							−0.375	−0.368	−0.205
							(0.01)**	(0.03)**	(0.10)*
Index of anticorruption legislation							−0.220	−0.163	−0.008
							(0.50)	(0.73)	(0.99)
Constant	1.738	2.058	3.932	1.914	2.928	1.842	3.036	2.995	3.510
	(0.00)***	(0.00)***	(0.00)***	(0.00)***	(0.00)***	(0.00)***	(0.00)***	(0.00)***	(0.00)***
Observations	23	23	23	23	23	23	23	23	23
R-squared	0.12	0.38	0.33	0.41	0.45	0.10	0.46	0.46	0.51

Sources: BEEPS 2005, *Doing Business in 2006* (World Bank 2006), World Bank's CPIA 2004, Rousso and Steves (2005) based on anticorruption laws and policies adopted between 1999 and 2002; World Development Indicators for GDP per capita in 2004.

Notes: Robust p values in parentheses: * significant at 10%; ** significant at 5%; *** significant at 1%. Regressions include all ECA countries except for Slovenia, Tajikistan, Turkey, Turkmenistan, and Uzbekistan for lack of at least one variable.

Table 9 Correlations between corruption outcomes and cross-cutting anticorruption policies

		Bribe frequency	Corruption as a problem doing business	Bribe tax	State capture
Measures of corruption outcomes	Corruption as a problem	0.67 (0.00)			
	Bribe tax	0.71 (0.00)	0.49 (0.00)		
	State capture	0.50 (0.00)	0.72 (0.00)	0.25 (0.18)	
Indexes of anticorruption activity	Anticorruption activity index	−0.28 (0.31)	**−0.44*** **(0.10)**	−0.29 (0.30)	−0.12 (0.67)
	Anticorruption strategy	**0.39** **(0.15)**	0.23 (0.41)	0.29 (0.29)	**0.53**** **(0.04)**
	Anticorruption policies	−0.02 (0.95)	0.04 (0.88)	**−0.39** **(0.15)**	0.21 (0.46)
Cross-cutting anticorruption policies and institutions	Political party financing	0.07 (0.80)	0.03 (0.93)	−0.05 (0.87)	0.18 (0.53)
	Asset monitoring	0.13 (0.64)	−0.02 (0.94)	0.00 (0.99)	**0.39** **(0.15)**
	Conflict of interest	**−0.42** **(0.12)**	**−0.49*** **(0.06)**	**−0.49*** **(0.06)**	**−0.43** **(0.11)**
	Financial and auditing controls	**−0.54**** **(0.04)**	**−0.61***** **(0.01)**	−0.30 (0.28)	−0.33 (0.22)
	Freedom of information	−0.10 (0.71)	−0.19 (0.49)	0.07 (0.80)	−0.33 (0.23)
	Immunities	−0.14 (0.63)	−0.32 (0.24)	−0.01 (0.96)	−0.30 (0.28)
	Public procurement	−0.33 (0.23)	**−0.41** **(0.13)**	−0.26 (0.36)	−0.11 (0.70)
Policies grouped by the part of government being controlled	Controls on the executive	**−0.56**** **(0.03)**	**−0.69***** **(0.00)**	−0.32 (0.25)	−0.29 (0.29)
	Controls on the legislature	−0.24 (0.39)	**−0.38** **(0.17)**	−0.27 (0.33)	−0.01 (0.96)
	Controls on the judiciary	−0.34 (0.21)	**−0.43** **(0.11)**	**−0.46*** **(0.09)**	−0.04 (0.88)

Source: Corruption measures are from BEEPS 2005; Anticorruption measures are from Dorhoi (2005).

Notes: The table shows simple correlations, with *p*-values in parentheses. There were 15 observations for each correlation. Correlations in bold are significant at least at the 20% level. Asterisks indicate higher levels of statistical significance: * significant at 10%; ** significant at 5%; *** significant at 1%. Anticorruption assessments are based on the status in 2003; Corruption measures are based on data in 2005.

Notes

1. These are simple averages across countries, such that each country has an equal weight.

2. For the four major dimensions of corruption, there is no significant difference between the average response of panel firms and nonpanel firms in either year. For corruption in specific sectors, there are some differences, although these are not always in the same direction. For some sectors, panel firms said more corruption and for other sectors less. (i) For fire and building inspections and environmental inspections, panel firms were somewhat more positive about the improvement, bringing the overall sample number up slightly. (ii) For taxes and courts, panel firms were somewhat more negative about the improvement, bringing the overall sample number down slightly. (iii) For courts, although the substantive conclusion is unaltered by the presence of the panel firms, it is interesting that the panel firms show a significantly worse assessment, while the overall sample shows no significant change. (iv) For the use of bribes to influence laws, panel firms were somewhat more negative about the improvement, bringing the overall sample number down slightly.

Bibliography

Ades and Di Tella. 1999. "Rents, competition and corruption." *American Economic Review* 89(4): 982–994.

Albania High Inspectorate for the Declaration and Audit of Assets. 2006. Website. http://www.hidaa.gov.al/en/declaration.htm (3/9/2006).

Anderson, James H., and Cheryl W. Gray. Forthcoming. "Reforming Judicial Systems in Transition Economies." *World Bank Economic Review.*

Anderson, James H., David S. Bernstein, and Cheryl W. Gray 2005. *Judicial Systems in Transition Economies—Assessing the Past, Looking to the Future.* Washington, D.C.: World Bank.

Bardhan, Pranab. 1997. *The Role of Governance in Economic Development: A Political Economy.* Washington, D.C.: OECD.

EBRD-World Bank Business Environment and Enterprise Performance Survey (BEEPS). 1999, 2002, 2005. European Bank for Reconstruction and Development and the World Bank (www.worldbank.org/eca/governance).

Center for Economic and Financial Research (CEFIR). 2005. *Monitoring the Administrative Barriers to Small Business Development in Russia.* November 2005. Moscow: CEFIR.

Coalition 2000. 2006. Website. http://www.anticorruption.bg/eng/coalition/about.htm.

Council of Europe, Group of States Against Corruption (GRECO). 2006. Website. http://www.greco.coe.int.

de Melo, Martha, Cevdet Denizer, Alan Gelb, and Stoyan Tenev. 1997. "Circumstances and Choice: The Role of Initial Conditions and Policies in Transition Economies." World Bank Policy Research Working Paper No. 1866. Washington, D.C.: World Bank.

Dorhoi, Monica. 2005. "Anti-Corruption Strategies and Fighting Corruption in Central and Eastern Europe." PhD Dissertation. Michigan State University.

European Bank for Reconstruction and Development. 2005. *Transition Report 2005—Business in Transition.* London: EBRD.

EU Monitoring and Advocacy Program (EUMAP). 2006. Website. http://www.eumap.org.

Evenett, Simon J., and Bernard Hoekman. 2005. "International Cooperation and the Reform of Public Procurement Policies." World Bank Policy Research Working Paper No. 3720. September 2005. Washington, D.C.: World Bank. Online at http://papers.ssrn.com/paper.taf?abstract_id=821424

Fischer, Stanley, and Ratna Sahay. 2000. "The Transition Economies after Ten Years." NBER Working Paper 7664. April 2000. Cambridge, MA: National Bureau of Economic Research (NBER).

Freedom House. Various years. *Nations in Transit*. Website: http://www.freedomhouse.org.

Grodeland, Ase Berit. 2005. "Informal Networks and Corruption in the Judiciary: Elite Interview Findings from the Czech Republic, Slovenia, Bulgaria, and Romania." Paper presented at the World Bank conference "New Frontiers of Social Policy," December 12–15, 2005, Arusha, Tanzania.

Hall, Robert E., and Charles Jones. 1999. "Why Do Some Countries Produce So Much More Output per Worker than Others?" *Quarterly Journal of Economics* 114(1): 83–116.

Hallward-Driemeier, Mary. 2006. "Who Survives? The Impact of Corruption, Competition and Property Rights across Firms." Processed. Washington, D.C.: World Bank.

Hameed, Farhan. 2005. "Fiscal Transparency and Economic Outcomes." IMF Working Paper WP/05/225, December 2005. Washington, D.C.: IMF.

Hellman, Joel, Geraint Jones, and Daniel Kaufmann. 2000. "Seize the State, Seize the Day—State Capture, Corruption, and Influence in Transition Economies." Policy Research Working Paper 2444. Washington, D.C.: World Bank.

Hessel, Marek, and Ken Murphy. 2004. "Stealing the State, and Everything Else—A Survey of Corruption in the Postcommunist World." Transparency International Working Paper. Online at http://ww1.transparency.org/working_papers/hessel/index.html.

Information Science for Democracy (INDEM). 2005. "Corruption process in Russia: level, structure, trends: Preliminary Report." Online at: http://www.indem.ru/en/publicat/2005diag_engV.htm (April 18, 2006).

Ivanova, Anna, Michael Keen, and Alexander Klemm. 2005. "The Russian 'Flat Tax' Reform." *Economic Policy* 20(43): 397–444.

Kaufmann, Daniel, Aart Kraay, and Massimo Mastruzzi. 2005. "Governance Matters IV. Governance Indicators for 1996-2004." Washington, D.C.: World Bank.

Kaufmann, Daniel, and Aart Kraay. 2002. "Growth Without Governance." *Economia* 3(1): 169–215.

Kaufmann, Daniel, Aart Kraay, and Pablo Zoido-Lobatón. 1999. "Governance Matters." Policy Research Working Paper No. 2196, Washington, D.C.: World Bank. Online at: http://www.worldbank.org/wbi/governance/pubs/govmatters.htm.

Knack, Stephen. 2006. ""Measuring Corruption in Eastern Europe and Central Asia: A Critique of Cross-Country Indicators." Processed. Washington, D.C.: World Bank.

Lambsdorff, Johann Graf. 2005. "Consequences and Causes of Corruption—What Do We Know From a Cross-Section of Countries?" Discussion Paper of the Economics Department, No. V-34-05. Passau: Passau University.

Mauro, Paolo. 1995. "Corruption and Growth." *Quarterly Journal of Economics* 110(3): 681–712.

Mungiu-Pippidi, Alina. Forthcoming. "Anticorruption as a Democratization Tool." *Journal of Democracy.*

North, Douglas. 1990. *Institutions, Institutional Change and Economic Performance.* Cambridge University Press.

Organisation for Economic Co-operation and Development (OECD). 2006. Website. http://www.oecd.org.

PlanConsult. 2003. "Interim Report II: Trade and Transport Facilitation in South East Europe Program: Provision of Consulting Services in User Survey Design and Implementation." Online at http://www.seerecon.org/ttfse/.

Polity IV Project. 2006. Website. http://www.cidcm.umd.edu/inscr/polity/#data.

Rauch, James E. 2001. "Leadership Selection, Internal Promotion, and Bureaucratic Corruption in Less Developed Polities." *Canadian Journal of Economics* 34(1): 240–258.

Rauch, James E., and Peter B. Evans. 2000. "Bureaucratic Structure and Bureaucratic Performance in Less Developed Countries." *Journal of Public Economics* 75: 49–71.

Romanian Coalition for a Clean Parliament. 2005. *A Quest for Political Integrity.* Bucharest: Polirom.

Rose, Richard. 2005. "Rogue States: A Bottom Up View From The Inside." World Peace Foundation Conference on Rogue States, Kennedy School of Government, Harvard. 28-30 April 2005.

Rousso, Alan, and Franklin Steves. 2005. "The Effectiveness of Anticorruption Programs: Preliminary Evidence from the Post-Communist Transition Countries." Processed. London: EBRD.

Spector, Bertram I., Michael Johnston, and Phyllis Dininio. 2005. "Learning Across Cases: Trends in Anticorruption Strategies." In Bertram I. Spector (eds.), *Fighting Corruption in Developing Countries: Strategies and Analysis*. Bloomfield, Connecticut: Kumarian.

Stability Pact Anticorruption Initiative. 2006. Website. http://www.spairslo.org.

Steves, Franklin, and Alan Rousso. 2003. "Anticorruption Programmes in Post-Communist Transition Countries and Changes in the Business Environment, 1999–2002." EBRD Working Paper No. 85. October. London: EBRD.

Svensson, Jakob. 2005. "Eight Questions about Corruption." *Journal of Economic Perspectives* 19(3): 19–42.

The Times (United Kingdom). February 21, 2001.

Transport Facilitation in Southeast Europe. Website. http://www.seerecon.org/ttfse/.

Transparency International. 2004. *Report on the Transparency International Global Corruption Barometer 2004*. Berlin: Transparency International.

———. 2005. *Report on the Transparency International Global Corruption Barometer 2005*. Berlin: Transparency International.

———. 2006. Website http://www.transparency.org.

Treisman, Daniel. 2000. "The Causes of Corruption: A Cross-National Study." *Journal of Public Economics* 76 (3): 399–457.

World Bank. 1997. *Helping Countries Combat Corruption—The Role of the World Bank*. Washington, D.C.: World Bank.

———. 2000. *Anticorruption in Transition: A Contribution to the Policy Debate* . Washington, D.C.: World Bank.

———. 2002. *Building Institutions for Markets*. World Development Report. Washington, D.C.: World Bank.

———. 2003. *Understanding Public Sector Performance in Transition Countries—An Empirical Contribution*. Washington, D.C.: World Bank.

———. 2004. *Anticorruption in Transition 2: Corruption in Enterprise-State Interactions in Europe and Central Asia 1999–2002 (ACT 2)*. Washington, D.C.: World Bank.

———. 2005a. *Administrative and Regulatory Reform in Russia: Addressing Potential Sources of Corruption*. Report Number: 36157- RU. Washington, D.C.: World Bank.

———. 2005b. *From Disintegration to Reintegration: Eastern Europe and the Former Soviet Union in International Trade*. Washington, D.C.: World Bank.

————. 2005c. *The Quest for Equitable Growth in the Slovak Republic: A World Bank Living Standards Assessment: Policy Note 2*. Washington, D.C.: World Bank.

————. 2006a. Website of the Poverty Reduction and Economic Management Unit for Europe and Central Asia. http://www.worldbank.org/eca/econ and governance section http://www.worldbank.org/eca/governance.

————. 2006b. *Enhancing Job Opportunities in Eastern Europe and the Former Soviet Union*. Washington, D.C.: World Bank.

————. 2006c. *Doing Business in 2006: Creating Jobs*. Washington, D.C.: World Bank (www.doingbusiness.org).

World Economic Forum. 2005. *Global Competitiveness Report 2005/2006*. http://www.weforum.org/ (May 11, 2006).